Client and Resource Management

The Innovative Design Firm

A Balanced Scorecard Approach

Part One –Introduction; People and Processes

Cliff S. Moser, AIA, MSQA

© 2009
ISBN 978-0-557-04978-3

...another Innovative Design Firm manual as published by **www.BeyondRedlines.com**

Contents

Management for the Innovative Design Firm

Management for the Innovative Design Firm

This book will show you how to build an architectural practice that will thrive and provide the owner and its staff with a successful and fulfilling career and living at any size. This book will show how to build a firm with a successful quality management program with meaningful performance and improvement measures. It will also identify new ways to examine and create performance, quality, and improvement measures. By utilizing the theories and tools behind balanced metrics and building a management program around them, a firm can begin to understand measure and improve the intangible activities of the organization. Using predefined balanced tools can help uncover the processes to support and link perspectives which will give an architectural firm opportunity to pursue sound growth, systemic efficiency, and performance improvement in a way that the traditional financial measures and benchmarking cannot.

The balanced scorecard breaks the firm into four perspectives. **People, Processes, Customers, and Financial**. By creating measures for these perspectives, the firm can identify the granularity of the steps in the activities it wants to measure and improve. Let's look at each perspective-

People

An Architectural Firm is a service business. In 2008, service businesses accounted for over 17% of adult employment in the US and Europe. Additionally, architecture is a *professional* service business. Professional services differ from other types of service firms in that their services are typically project-based and are performed in direct

collaboration with a stakeholder. Additionally, the professional firm's assets are not

tied-up in inventory or equipment, but in its staff's expertise. Our most valuable assets

are not machinery or buildings, but those assets which get up from their desks every

night to go home. Therefore, a firm's asset building ability is based on the success of

attracting, motivating, and managing these peripatetic resources. An enthusiastic,

excited and engaged staff is necessary for any firm to win exciting work and retain

rewarding client relationships, as well as manage its processes and financial

requirements.

Processes

An architecture firm uses processes to produce its project work. There are the

drawing, drafting and modeling processes. There are the billing and invoicing processes,

the marketing and business development processes. There are the processes linked to

hiring, training and promoting staff. Processes within a firm create success or failure for

the other perspectives. A balanced management approach focuses on reviewing the

firm's existing processes as well as creating new processes, to support its people,

customer and financial needs.

Customers

An architecture firm can't exist without clients. These are the firm's customers

for which the firm creates its projects for. But the firm also has customers beyond its clients. While the narrow view of customer is someone who *pays* for goods or services, a quality-focused organization will recognize a customer as someone who *receives* deliverables or services from another. Therefore we have *external* customers in the form of clients, but also as contractors, code agencies, and consultants. Internal to our firm we have customers who depend on us for deliverables. Such as the billing staff who need our timesheets, or the HR staff who need our vacation requests, and the project manager who needs our marked-up floor plans. The customer perspective recognizes and measures interactions with all customers; internal and external. The architecture firm needs robust customer metrics in order for it to support the people, processes and financial needs of the firm.

Financial

Finally, the firm needs money. These are the fees and billings, the expenditures and outlays that keep a business operating. However, a balanced financial perspective should do more than just track cash input and output. Metrics in the financial perspective help the firm to focus on finding (and retaining) clients that support the processes and people and continued growth of the organization. It should also help the firm recognize its strengths and weaknesses within the other perspectives and provide balanced guidance for becoming profitable.

What is a balanced scorecard? A Balanced Scorecard is an organizational performance and improvement system that helps a firm identify and measure management metrics beyond financial performance.

The Balanced Scorecard

In the early 1990s, Robert Kaplan and David Norton developed a new approach to strategic management. Based on the premise that intangible, or knowledge-based, assets—employees, volunteers, information technology, image—are increasingly important to an organization's success. They called it a balanced scorecard in that it not only measures financial outcomes, but also balances the financial perspective with employee, business process and customer perspectives.

Additionally, a balanced scorecard provides a method for aligning day to day business activities to organizational strategy. Through a balanced scorecard, the organization's vision and mission statement can be translated into specific and calculable goals. And balanced performance measures are established to monitor the organization's success in achieving those goals.

Through a scorecard, the firm's vision is translated into operational goals, and linked to studio or departmental (and even to individual) performance.

Through a scorecard a plan for business processes is outlined, and the organization's strategy is modified based on feedback of the metrics of the perspectives.

The balanced scorecard process involves viewing the organization from four perspectives, developing measurements to gauge performance and analyzing data relative to each perspective:

The **People** or learning and growth perspective – measures reflecting an organization's learning curve

The **Process** perspective – measures reflecting performance of key business processes.

Customer or stakeholder perspective – measures directly impacting customers and customer satisfaction

The Financial perspective – measures reflecting financial performance

The four perspectives of the scorecard allow for a balance between:

-Short- and long-term objectives

-Outcomes desired and the performance-drivers of those outcomes

-Objective and subjective measures

In a perfect planning cycle, the balanced scorecard is derived from the organization's strategic plan; the strategy map is derived from the balanced scorecard; and the operating budget stems from all three.

This book focuses on the day to day management of the organization, in order to maintain alliance and symmetry with the firm's strategic scorecard.

This introduction identifies ways to integrate these measurement techniques into a firm's traditional performance and quality tracking systems and to begin discussing strategies and goals with staff and customers.

Creating a Balanced Performance and Quality Management System for the Architecture Firm

Creating a Balanced Performance and Quality Management System for the Architecture Firm

Traditional performance metrics are typically only financial. An architectural firm will measure its survival and growth based on fee, current projects, and backlog. Other financial measures may include a percentage mix of direct and indirect labor, projected and actual work, and the quantity and types of clients served. While they are important, financial metrics only measure a portion of the firm's real value. And most traditional financial measures are lagging indicators. As they measure only the past, they are completely unable to capture and quantify the transient and non financial assets of the firm such as client satisfaction, staff training and expertise, innovation, or pricing to value.

The original Balanced Scorecard sought to remedy this by creating metrics through four business perspectives. They are described as perspectives because they present opportunities for different viewpoints or lenses into and outside of the organization.

The four perspectives are:

People, Processes, Customers and Financial.

...the first perspective

People

As stated earlier, its staff is the architectural firm's most valuable assets. Activities based on attracting, training, mentoring, rewarding and retaining its staff will help a firm thrive. Excited, engaged and cognitively diverse staff will, in turn, help the firm attract and retain exciting clients and projects. Successful business development isn't simply realized by meeting with potential clients and handing out brochures and business cards.

The successful organization understands that prudent treatment of its staff will create satisfied client interactions and in turn support growth. Tools within the people perspective validate that fact that systems, not staff, cause failure. The people perspective helps the firm understand that it creates a work environment where staff can excel or languish. Circumstances are powerful determinants of behavior. Therefore the people measure is the first and most important perspective.

Processes

Processes are the functions a firm utilizes to provide its services. The Process perspective encompasses all of the activities involved in running a successful firm-- from marketing to drawing, from project to office management. All are processes.

Quality guru Dr. W. Edwards Deming identified processes and systems as the foundation for management and organizational transformation. His theory focuses the fact that processes within an architectural firm are interrelated-- they are overlapping and discontinuous actions of the organization.

In implementing a balanced scorecard a firm will analyze processes that should be eliminated or modified.

Knowledge-based processes.

There are two types of organizational knowledge. The first type of knowledge is *explicit knowledge*. This is the easy-to-find knowledge found in the firm's forms, manuals, documentation, files and other accessible sources. It is also the knowledge that can be easily transmittable in formal or systematic language.

The second type of knowledge is the *implicit knowledge* which resides within the firm's staff as its experience, skills and expertise. Implicit knowledge is intangible and difficult to access. It is also hard to measure and incorporate into the firm's processes. Implicit knowledge is personal, context specific, and hard to formalize and communicate. A firm without the proper processes and protocols for capturing and leveraging this knowledge doesn't even know what it doesn't know.

Therefore, stated in balanced scorecard terms, if an architectural firm has the right staff (people perspective) doing the right things (process perspective), then its clients (customer perspective) will be delighted and it will get more business (financial perspective).

Customers.

The customer perspective asks that a firm recognizes how it identifies and serves its customers. In a balanced scorecard, customers are identified as external and internal. External customers are clients, owners, regulatory agencies and contractors. Internal customers are consultants, suppliers, firm staff, and inter-team members. Project-based organization relationships are confined to teams involved in the discrete activities of the project. Traditional long-term, supply-chain factory-based customer relationship issues like trust, commitment, and reciprocity are absent. Team members rely instead on rigid contractual conditions which typically frame and codify relationships.

Balanced metrics helps the firm understand and manage its complex network of customers. The customer perspective focuses on external customer fee and pricing, as well as deliverable and service issues. For internal customer issues, this perspective helps the firm align and manage staff, as well as consultant and supplier satisfaction.

The customer perspective also focuses on successful client delivery. This includes post-design or post-occupancy reviews, in which the firm may discover that there are several consumer requirements missing or poorly thought-out within the completed design.

Financial

The fourth and final perspective is financial. An architectural firm's financial measures are traditional simple balance-sheet metrics. Salaries and rent make up liabilities, with receivables and cash flow comprising assets. The firm funds itself through working capital, cash flow, and retained earnings. There are typically low net tangible asset values such as office equipment and computers; some of the more expensive equipment is leased. With virtually no depreciation and low capital expenditures, the typical firm shows a balance sheet that's deceptively small in comparison to its actual revenues.

The ability to generate prepaid expenses or retainers from booked projects and generate interest earnings from these deposits is critical. A backlog of booked projects allows a firm to plan resources. The only leading indicator is projected and actual sales.

Work in progress (WIP) is a leading indicator of potential trouble. WIP is the firm's excess inventory in the form of design or construction drawings. Improperly understood and measured, WIP has a severe negative potential for incremental or total write-off at the end of the project. Undercapitalized firms with big gaps between accumulated WIP and receipt of collection payments can cause cash flow and payroll problems

Balanced metrics for the financial perspective provide new pricing and money tools.

Using Balanced Scorecard metrics helps identify tools and processes necessary to enable a firm to build a narrative of what the firm should know about its business, its strategies, and its mission, vision and goals. These tools help clarify the reason for the organization. They also provide direction in creating mission, vision and goals. They allow managers to identify strategies and goals that will allow them to build a better, sustainable organization. Balanced metrics also formalize clear operating system guidelines in order for a firm to change or modify the goals that already exist within a project-based adhocracy environment.

Before we start to implement a balanced scorecard, we need to outline the typical structure of a design firm.

Adhocracy

All architecture firms are project-based organizations, operating to the individual requirements of a collaboration of diversely trained specialists. This team comes together to perform complex, non-routine tasks around the creation and delivery of specific service and deliverables for a specific customer, or client. The organizational hierarchy of an architectural firm organically evolves in order to support its projects.

The firm's projects need resources and an organization for support. That organization is a patchwork of management styles and is develops situationally for what works best. It's flatly hierarchical, and fleetingly ad-hoc.

To best describe this organization, we use the term "**Adhocracy**."

Unlike the traditional bureaucracy, with its layers of command, control, checks and balances, an **adhocracy** works perfectly for a project-based architecture firm in that it allows the quick creation of a highly organic organization, with minimal leadership built on serving a single project.

This ad-hoc structure supports the peer-based professionals in the firm; the architects and project managers, creating a reporting structure that facilitates an organization's changing project demands and goals. However the lack of hierarchy in this management style doesn't allow for scalability.

Because there are no clear subordinate relationships, ambiguities develop over authority and responsibilities. Adhocracies tend to suffer from numerous internal team conflicts. It is nearly impossible to compartmentalize roles and standardize tasks. Adhocracies also inhibit the transfer of knowledge. When a project is completed, there is no mechanism to capture, retain or promulgate the knowledge gained during the course of the project with the rest of the organization.

Smaller project teams function better within an adhocracy, because communication within an adhocracy is informal, dynamic and serial, larger teams do not encourage mutual learning and flexibility of their members. This *functional adhocracy* is made up of numerous project teams, which need a designated leader or 'manager' in order to understand, distill, and delegate the work. The firm's "project managers" run the functional adhocracy.

However, in order for this agile **functional adhocracy** to operate successfully utilizing all the organization's tools and resources, it needs the help of the firm's administrative staff. This administrative team, as overhead costs to the organization, is typically protected from the projects' needs and demands, and is tasked to provide organization to the project-induced chaos of the **functional adhocracy**. Indeed, this separate team functions as an *administrative adhocracy*, a completely separate and distinct organization within the firm.

Because the professional team's functional adhocracy is completely free of structure and form, the **administrative adhocracy** becomes an ultra-bureaucracy in an attempt to balance order into the anarchy. In a role familiar to all functional adhocracy members within architecture firms, the **administrative adhocracy** creates absolutely rigid standards and controls forcing the functional adhocracy to yield to the requirements in order to receive its needed resources. Processes and controls within the administrative adhocracy are standardized and demanding –there is no room for flexibility or changes. This dichotomy develops in order to counter the lawlessness of the **functional adhocracy**.

This collision is a familiar one to the functional operations. It occurs at the intersection of firm-wide organizational procedures-- the extrinsic knowledge base of forms, manuals, time reporting, project setup, and equipment requirements. This intersection includes timesheets, expense reports, telephone system codes, copier access numbers, and the arcane filing requirements that are the result of **administrative adhocracy's** attempt to corral the outlaw nature of the functional adhocracies of professional staff.

If this office polarization wasn't enough, there is an additional organization within the firm. This organization belongs to the Executives. Executives don't comfortably exist within the functional adhocracy, as they are not tied to project requirements, nor are they completely within the administrative adhocracy arena. The Executives exist within a small tightly knit command and control pyramid at the top of the organization which we call the **Executive Adhocracy**.

The **executive adhocracy** dictates the rules to the systems below. While executives in the firm are created out of the **functional adhocracy** (as they are licensed professionals who worked as project staff earlier in their career), they now help provide structure and protocols to the administrative adhocracy. Being hierarchically above admin, they don't have to play by the same rules they have helped develop for the functional adhocracy staff. Executives don't usually worry about copier codes, time sheet requirements, and filing requirements, because they have their own admin staff that does that for them.

Therefore one of the roles of a balanced scorecard is to remind the **executive adhocracy** of the **functional** and **administrative adhocracies** operating below it.

Before embarking on the path to a balanced scorecard, the firm should map out how each management group-- the **executive, administrative or functional adhocracy**-- will utilize its role for the collecting, managing and reporting the metrics of the balanced scorecard. In its balancing role, the scorecard helps the **administrative adhocracy** create the forms and protocols with the **functional adhocracy**. For balanced management to be a success each group must be integrate with the other for gathering and reporting the scorecard metrics.

That integration begins by bringing the adhocracies together to map out the future of the firm that will be enabled by the scorecard perspectives and metrics. This starts with:

Mission and Vision statements

Please don't close the book.

I'm the first to acknowledge that mission and visioning can be a lame process in the hands of most firms. And this book doesn't present a new how-to guide on proper mission and visioning, however, properly established and executed, dynamic mission and vision statements are required to map out the future direction of the firm. And mission and vision are the initial steps to integrating the adhocracies.

Plainly stated, a mission statement describes why the firm *is,* and the vision statement describes what the firm wants to **be**.

Mission and vision are used to create the framework to support the balanced management as well as strategies and goals of the firm. Traditional mission and visioning sessions diminish the energy that truly muscular and resilient statements should contain to help create a narrative path for balanced scorecard success for the firm.

Creating successful balanced systems are necessary to align the feuds that can exist within the firm. However, during mission and visioning the metrics required to measure success are typically treated as secondary activities and left back at the office while executives and high-level functional staff builds mission and vision off-site. The admin and remaining functional staff back at the ranch often can't get their arms around the rhetoric that comes back, and contains no references about how to attain that success, and no mechanisms to measure it.

Mission and Visioning should occur in the office, around a conference table with everyone involved. Front line functional staff as well as admin (including the receptionist) should participate in developing mission and vision statements that help a firm define what it is and what it wants to be through the perspectives of people, processes, customers, and finance.

If a firm were to focus on enhancing **customer quality**, a mission/vision should state:

...support and enhancement of the firm's opportunity for developing a successful client base by providing high levels of technical competence, high demand requirements matched with prudent risk-taking. In this perspective, the role key clients' play in promoting design innovation should be recognized by the firm. A firm's experienced client base should be identified and leveraged by the firm as the main institution leader in stimulating construction and design innovation.

...help build strategic relationships with consultants, regulatory agencies, and contractors within the firm's specialized industry.

...create innovative and integrated approaches to construction projects, in response to the fragmentation of the industry arising from the one-off nature of most projects and the proliferation of smaller and smaller subcontractors.

A mission/vision statement focused on the **people perspective** should:

...improve knowledge-capture, -flow, and -transfer within each team as well as the whole organization by creating processes which track and contain decision-making. This offsets the disadvantages of production based on temporary project-related coalitions of firms.

For the process perspective

...integrate of project experience into continuous business processes to limit the loss of implicit knowledge between projects.

...promote innovation procurement systems, including partnering to enhance cooperative problem-solving, the adoption of non-standard solutions, and equitable allocation of risk.

For the financial perspective

...build up organizational resources, including developing a culture supportive of innovation, enhancing in-house technical competence, supporting innovation champions, and developing an effective innovation strategy.

Most importantly, a balanced scorecard **does not** re-create an organization through re-engineering. It operates as a vehicle that helps the architectural firm understand itself and then assists the firm in creating strategies for sustenance and growth.

The balanced scorecard helps the firm find metrics available within existing processes and then provides tools to use those metrics for the management and improvement of these processes. This means that the organization implementing a balanced scorecard needs only to add a collection and reporting function in order to begin. This is not a series of measures that quickly overwhelm the firm. It's a system that helps focus direction and meaning with all of the firm's stakeholders.

Cultural Shift

However, the cultural shift required within a firm to implement and maintain a scorecard cannot be discounted. Most firms capture and monitor only a small amount of performance-related information. Project metrics report small measures such as submittal turnaround times or change orders. Initiative and organizational metrics may capture data regarding employee turnover or new professional registrations or memberships, but typically that information is static and lagging, and soon discarded. In order to reap the benefit and usefulness of a scorecard in lieu of familiar measures, there must be an organizational push for excellence. Asking the architectural firm to identify and monitor new metrics such as client satisfaction and firm expertise will be a difficult task if its past measures of success were simple and meaningless.

Key Performance Indicators

Therefore a firm should develop key performance indicators (KPIs) in order to begin developing performance metrics. KPIs allow a firm to develop new indicators or apply existing industry recognized metrics when they create a scorecard. In the following chapters we will suggest KPIs for each discussion item. Here are some example KPIs that could be developed for each perspective.

KPIs for the **People Perspective**

-KPI -Learning and innovation –ability to capture new design skills from experience in major projects and clients.

KPI -Staff professional development –percentage and ratio of employees studying for selected registration –LEED, ARE's, IID, CSI, those that are registered and those that are taking the exam.

KPIs for the **Process Perspective**

KPI -Integrating design into objectives –translating business objectives into design goals, and elaborating for the purpose of measuring and improving. This step is essential to ensure that design is integrated into the firm.

KPI -Internal design processes –project management and business support, including developing leadership and communications skills essential for project effectiveness within the architectural firm.

KPIs for the **Customer Perspective**

KPI –Client Needs – Understanding and satisfying existing demands for simple and radical designs, as well as anticipating future needs. Ultimately, this shapes the client's perceptions about the design ability of the company.

KPI –External Design Processes – Managing consultants, contractors and clients during the design process, as well as developing organization-wide capabilities in partnering arrangements to improve cross-firm team and organizational performance.

KPIs for the **Financial Perspective**

The firm can use traditional metrics –staff billability, revenue per project manager, etc. But to really embrace balanced metrics, the firm should try to stretch, and try new goals.

Rent per Principal –set a target number

Expertise –number of professional memberships, etc.

Summary

A balanced scorecard helps the architectural firm identify and measure its existing *intangible* assets and liabilities, as well identify and develop new performance indicators. These new balanced metrics should also help the firm capture its intrinsic/extrinsic project and organizational knowledge. What may be more a more difficult process in developing a scorecard in determining what to measure, is to learn how to ignore the interesting, but unimportant, performance data. The following chapters will outline how to develop meaningful metrics from identified processes within each perspective.

As an organization, the architectural firm's business model should include change. The role of an architecture firm as a successful for-profit organization is to earn fees and make money, and to plan for a long and sustaining growth model. As we've seen in the past few years, a firm must also be able to anticipate and adjust to change. Change within the industry, change within its client base, and change in processes, and staffing requirements. A scorecard can adjust and leverage the change to the betterment of the firm. Before implementing a scorecard, potential pitfalls to avoid include:

Balanced Metric Pitfalls

1)   **Premature links to management processes** – if the scorecard isn't carefully planned with each required link outlined and endorsed, the required balanced metrics will wither from lack of resources and data.

2)   **Lack of cascading through the firm** – the three adhocracies of executives, administration, and functional must understand what a scorecard is and what function it will perform. Each member of the organization, whether actively or peripherally involved with the balanced management effort must know how they will be affected (and what they will be expected to do) for the scorecard.

3)   **Terminology -** Buzzwords and flavor-of-the-month management ideas will destroy any initiative. If the terminology of the project cannot be aligned with the existing knowledge and vernacular of the firm, the program will be perceived to be an out-of-touch management overlay system doomed to failure.

4)   **No new measures** started as part of the scorecarding activity. If the organization

continues to do what it was doing before the scorecard, then why implement it? And why should the firm and its staff support it?

5)   **Inconsistent management practices**. The scorecard must align existing disparate organizational management practices already in place. If a single but important process is forgotten, left out or not aligned or revised with the introduction of the scorecard, then it will highlight the organization's inconsistency and arbitrariness.

6)   **Poor Timing**. The implementation must match the change, crisis, opportunity or strategy that the scorecard is trying to improve.

7)   **No clear objectives** for the introduction of the balanced scorecard. A scorecard cannot be implemented without clear, communicable, and understandable goals. A firm's front-line drafting and administrative staff must understand the goals of a scorecard *completely* and be able to describe them *simply*.

8)   **No strategy**. How is the scorecard going to help achieve the goals outlined in item seven? A clear strategy for attainment and sustainment must be clearly outlined.

9)   **Lack of training and education**. This can be the easiest but also deadliest omission for the implementation of a successful scorecard. A rollout without the

appropriate level of training and education will doom balanced management to the "I-already-have-too-much-to-do-and-we've-already-tried-this-kind-of-stuff-before" syndrome. If the organization cannot afford a budget for training in association with the costs necessary for collecting and reporting the new data collected for the scorecard, then the entire process should be postponed or rethought.

10)	**No executive sponsorship**. The executive adhocracy must champion and sponsor the move to balanced management. If there is no active executive support, then the scorecard is seen as a waste of important resources. The firm's executive team must believe in and support the change, offering to go the extra mile themselves if necessary to guarantee its success.

Balanced Metrics Implementation

Balanced scorecard implementation should be a major transition, a sea change, a paradigm shift, a burning platform that changes the existing organizational landscape. A successful scorecard cannot be introduced gradually. Big changes are more painful but last longer. A firm's staff respect bold moves and are more likely to participate in the implementation if it is perceived to be big and important enough to withstand attempts to counter it. Make the change big, but appropriate. A successful scorecard helps unite the operational and administrative adhocracy.

Work sheets (I've copied simple cells for starting a monthly balanced metric)

Wt	Perspective	Metric	Requirement	Goal	Achieved	Subtotal	Total %
0.5	People	Training	Weekly training metrics	100%	85%	0.425	
1	Processes	Internal	Weekly process metrics	100%	95%	0.95	
1.5	Customer	Client touch	Weekly customer metrics	100%	95%	1.425	
2	Financial	Contractor models	Weekly financials	100%	95%	1.9	
6						5.70	95%
	The following table describes the current payout:	Score		Payout			Annualized
		0 - 49.9%		$ -			$ -
		50 - 59.9%		$ -			$ -
		60 - 69.9%		$ -			$ -
		70 - 84.9%		$ 100.00			$ 1,200.00
		85 - 94.9%		$ 300.00			$ 3,600.00
		> 95%		$ 500.00			$ 6,000.00

PEOPLE

People

Narrative

In the regional of one large national firm, I had the task of creating a staffing schedule. Each week I would update the resource plan by asking each project manager their project staff projections. After a few months of this exercise, I realized that management was treating some staff as "stand-by" personnel. These staffers were not architects, but talented artists, highly skilled in watercolor renderings. When that particular skill wasn't needed, these staff members were assigned to trivial tasks, like filing and storeroom reorganization, while waiting to put brush and paint to paper. The BSC identified that the firm management was underutilizing this resource 80% of the time in order to leverage the remaining 20%. The resulting "staff satisfaction" metric languished abysmally. It became evident that it was only a matter of time before these marginalized artists would set out to find more challenging jobs with career-building potential. Essentially, they were well-positioned to leverage themselves right out of the firm.

Understanding how to measure intangible assets like staff experience, project history and its knowledge base allows an architectural firm to leverage metrics into goals and strategies. This is the function of the balanced scorecard. A scorecard of aligned performance targets and metrics, supported by a determined mission and vision will create a well-planned, smoothly-ordered, and sustainable organization poised for growth.

Narrative

People are the intangibles assets that run the organization. Currently our in our architectural world, people are changing from the clients and staff that all the management books were written about 15 years ago. We're changing to the new world of GenXr's, Millennials, and soon, Generation Z, who will work alongside the old timers (these ain't your grandfathers' drawings,-or your grandfather's management,- or firm) who are still in the thick of running things.

People Perspective Metrics–

Management, staff and stakeholder concerns are the enablers and promoters of the other three measures: processes, customers and financials. People-based metrics in a scorecard measure the firm's greatest and most intangible assets. How can the architectural firm utilize a BSC to best empower and manage its creative staff?

In order to understand how a BSC helps the organization understand and leverage its People perspective, the firm must understand the characteristics and deeper purpose of its staff. To assemble and manage the best possible staff, a firm must also:

Expect and prepare for failure –the firm should create an environment in which the best route to job security is by working to outdo the company's competition—not by planning it safe. The organization should focus energy on developing new processes and new ways to solve problems, not by worrying about staff failure.

As such, the firm should identify errors but keep repercussions small when conquest-oriented staff makes mistakes. **If your staff doesn't fail once or twice on a project, it's not taking enough risks**. Staff should be promoted based on lessons learned and sharing of their failures. The human resource objective is to develop staff with continuous years of experience, not the first year's experience repeated over and over.

Create an Us vs. Them atmosphere, not with co-workers but with the competition. Openly identify and review what your competition is doing. If a new hire comes from another firm, ask them to make a presentation on how their old firm won projects and treated their staff and customers. The idea is not to institute a gripe session, but to create a 'reverse engineering' analysis that can tap into the lessons learned from competing organizations.

Create, support, and sustain a start-up mentality for the organization. There should be a sense of urgency that the business must succeed and become sustainable. The firm should make it everyone's responsibility to understand and manage all costs and try to add value to all processes. For example, if five people are thought to be required to complete a project, talk to the team and plan to start staffing with four. Although understaffing is already a tacit resource model in many architecture firms; planned understaffing is undertaken with the intent to review and improve existing processes.

T-Shaped People

In hiring, a firm should look for "T-shaped people". These are staff that have skills and knowledge that is both singularly deep as well as broad. These workers are experts in specific technical areas but they are also aware of the systemic impact of their tasks as well as their work in general. The vertical stroke of the T measures their knowledge of a particular discipline while the horizontal stroke indicated their awareness of how their discipline interacts with others.

T-shaped skills surface anywhere problem solving is required. These skills facilitate expertise action across various functional knowledge bases, as well as creative broader based knowledge at the intersection. Staff possessing appropriate T-skills can shape their knowledge to fit the problem at hand rather than insist that the problem appear or be presented in a familiar and recognizable form. With their wide experience in applying functional discipline knowledge, T-shaped people are capable of convergent synergistic thinking.

Team members with T-shaped skill are the structure of the people perspective systems-focused balanced scorecard. Where does the typical architectural firm find them? In most organizations T-shaped skills are not created as a deliberate policy, but emerge because individuals have been willing to risk pursuing a somewhat marginal career.

Most formal organizational incentives encourage "I-shaped" skills, the deep function expertise represented by the "T" stem. As a result, this particular individual is driven deeper into his or her expertise, which the organization continually draws on and rewards. At the same time, the organization provides no clear career path for those who want to top off the stem with a broad range of applications.

But creative problem solving requires both skills. **System-focused companies create staff with T-shaped skills by carefully shaping and guiding individual careers to provide exposure to a broad range of experiences.** Thus, designers must know about contractor RFIs and submittals, construction administrators must be able to create conceptual designs for charrette presentations, and administrative staff must understand the fits and starts of project workplans.

Willing Volunteers

Additionally, firm staff should be treated like **creative and willing volunteers** who are tied to the firm not by money but by commitment to the firm's aims and purposes. Creative staff wants and expects to be part of the organization's administration and management processes, actively helping set goals and assisting with the monitoring and reporting. The commitment of creative people is highly contingent; they are motivated the same way volunteers are motivated. Creative staff does it for the challenge, the responsibility, respect and recognition, as well as the pay. They join a firm to work with other creative people and exciting projects. **A firm should rely on an employee's intrinsic motivations, seducing the intangible factor, while keeping an eye on the extrinsic motivations, making sure they treat staff as loyal internal customers.**

At the bottom of this creative staff food chain is the "still-in" or "right-out-of-school" intern. An experienced firm understands that this Millennial designer is different from other professional employees in the firm. As an architect, this employee is definitely different from other professional service firm workers like accountants and lawyers.

When the economy was roaring, freshly graduated accountants and lawyers could move into a heavy extrinsically compensated workplace environment and immediately move into the middle class (money-wise). Indeed, newly-graduated architects have the same debt burden as other professionals, but our profession in good and bad-times, typically pays fresh-out-of school staff, pocket change in relation to what lawyers and accountants make.

In leveraging this new-but-unskilled professional, without resorting to money, money money, the firm can utilize a scorecard to promote and measure treatment of this individual. Most new staff are looking for a short-term arrangement which gives them some real-world experience and adds flesh to the bones of their resume. If the job grows beyond that target of resume-fodder and actually creates long-term links and relationships, then it is value added beyond expectations.

However, if the work only meets expectations, then the employee is actually being prepared to move on. As identified earlier, the successful employer should understand and treat its workers as fleeting assets. All architectural firms nurture their success on the transplanted assets borrowed from other firms. A creative workforce can be incredibly loyal, working long hours just to be involved in a particular project, understanding that money is secondary. Unfortunately, the firm also has the opportunity to negatively capitalize from this dedication.

Newly Minted Professional Staff

As professional staff, this newly minted typically receives no paid overtime. Therefore, if a staff member works a 50-hour week in lieu of a traditional 40-hour week, that adds up to a 25% free donation in extra time for the project and the firm. Over the course of a year a 50-hour employee is working an equivalent of 3 months for free for the architectural firm. If the same employee works a 60-hour week, he/she is donating an extra 50% of paid time to the project and firm.

The potential for abuse is tremendous, and staff treated in this fashion for an extended period of time should be expected to frequently turnover. Additionally, this kind of behavior skews the budgets for actual-to-scheduled costs, **since 50% of the work is being done for free**, the firm should be prepared to adjust the budget or hire one and a half people for every individual staff member who leaves.

In accounting for this, the firm should try to design people perspective metrics that are not just for the functional adhocracy of drafting, design and professional staff. Measures should include the administrative adhocracy of accounting, IT, and marketing staff as well. These people are also T-Shaped, as they have a strong down-stroke in their discipline, but are drawn to working for an architecture firm in the same way that professional staffers are. Though they could typically find work within other industries and professions, this staff is attracted to the architectural field to be close to the creative people that work there. In fact, the administrative staff consists of creative people with the same interests and passions as those professionals within the firm. These people are independent creative self-starters who enjoy the flexible conditions of an architectural firm.

Traditionally, a large and specialized staff once performed this work; it is now completed by a small and cross-functionally trained workforce. Each member of this non-professional group develops into ad hoc managers. Soon, they are using existing communications to channel flows of information, devising and setting up new systems, and making difficult management decisions on the fly. This is why they choose to work and stay employed within a firm. This staff contributes more than organization, intelligence, or computer skills. This staff adds intangible assets of creative value to the organization just as much as its design professionals do.

People Perspective KPIs

One of the goals of the people perspective of the balanced scorecard should be to devise metrics which identify and measure particular KPIs 1) retention of staff, the 2) attraction of new talented individuals, as well as the 3) generation of positive metrics for the processes, customers, and financial perspectives.

For **retention**, the firm could develop an orientation metric. In this measure, each new employee is assigned each new employee a sponsor or buddy, a peer already with the company who can be a guide through the machinations of the office for a few days while the new employee completes the required paperwork and settles in. The objective behind an orientation metric is to ensure that the new staff member is not left standing or just thrown headlong into the pool. The buddy has lunch with him, walks him around the office, and helps him feel connected and part of the organization. In the orientation metric the firm would provide a project number for orientation that the new employee and buddy would charge to. Success would be measured by spending all the hours identified and assigned to new staff orientation. This mitigates the fact that, too often, professional employee integration is not considered a requirement of the office. The metric helps both the new and existing staff feel as if they are part of a team with a clear directions and defined goals.

The office orientation metric can be considered as just one of the first steps in a balanced scorecard for staff sustenance. The cost of constantly hiring and training workers can be unsustainable for a firm that wants to remain competitive. Just as personal problems cascade through the lives of employees, they eventually cascade into the organizations which employ them.

Align Perspectives

Thus, building robust scorecards help align the people perspective and assist the organization by integrating the function and administrative adhocracies. A scorecard help create systems where as many decisions as possible are made by the people closest to a particular situation. Instead of assuming that all problems need to be filtered up the hierarchy and every solution back down again, the organization should trust the staff to create workable and efficient solutions. However, if all decisions have to be made by upper management, it silo's the adhocracies and frustrates decision-making. The executive, manager, boss or a small group of managers at the top should not dictate requirements.

The profession should strive to embrace ideas of inclusiveness broad enough to include the **administrative adhocracy** outlined above. Collaborative empowerment is often confused with the quest for a consensus. However, the search for consensus encourages lowest common denominator solutions that try not to offend instead of building an exciting team. Rather than fostering the free exchange of conflicting views, consensus-driven groups trade in the familiar and squelch debate. Unless people know what the true state of affairs is, it's unlikely they'll make the right decisions. A balanced scorecard should make these decisions transparent. This means the organization should first be honest about performance and expectations.

Creating a high performance organization goes hand in hand with creating a high-trust organization. In a high trust organization, the firm explains its business matters fully, modifies its flows of communication accordingly, develop sets of shared goals, build teams rather than concentrating on individuals, offer rewards rather than punishment, and stay in touch with what's happening on the floor and workstation. It helps a firm pay attention to the concerns, issues, *the* personal issues of the employees. It assists the firm create meaningful roles for its functional and administrative employees.

Additional People KPIs

In creating meaningful metrics for the people perspective, the firm should leverage its mission, vision, and goals and focus on measures for functional and administrative staff retention, referrals, staff development, and training.

People measures could include outstanding number of applications for employment, percentage of promotions from project architect to project manager, or a sort of applications based on diversity. Other measures could include percentage of professional registrations and specialty certification such as CSI, or LEED among staff and associates.

Confirming important issues outlined earlier, another useful measure could be the percentage of membership in professional organizations outside of the design and construction industry. Create metrics that build the required T-shaped staff.

Below are some tables with suggested leading and lagging indicators, and proposed metrics.

Leading Indicators

Leading indicators in the people perspective should focus on long-term staff and management planning. For example, in addition to recruiting efforts at the local architectural or design school, the healthcare architectural firm might look to provide information and workshops at local nursing schools, or at universities with healthcare business programs. A leading indicator would be the number of meetings held with disparate groups.

Lagging Indicators

Lagging indicators for the people perspective might measure existing percentage of identity, gender, and racial diversity in the office.

The table below shows how to start building an initiative BSC with appropriate perspective objectives and lag and lead measures.

Initiative	Perspective	Objective	Lag Measure	Lead Measure	Target
Build Cognitive Diversity	Financial	Build diverse teams into fee breakdowns	•	•	•
	Customer	Introduce Diverse Team to Clients	•	•	•

	Processes	Integrate new staff through existing studios			
	People	Hire cognitively diverse staff	Resumes of currently employed staff	Hiring	% of staff outside of profession or with multiple degrees

The people perspective goes beyond the solitary island of the architectural firm. In the new integrated project delivery (IPD) realm the owner's and contractor's staff are part of the people perspective as early project team members who are introduced to the chaos of adhocracies.

For example, the billing **administrative adhocracy** may clash with the **functional adhocracy's** new integrated requirements of project deliverables. The **executive adhocracy** will wring its hands wondering why there are these communication problems. The goal of building a high performing project team may seem impossible if the team can't agree on goals and responsibilities or even the format of the meeting minutes.

In the next few chapters, we will look at People perspective focused tools that can be utilized to help the Innovative Firm plan for sustainable management success.

Appreciative Inquiry and Project Partnering

Appreciative Inquiry and Project Partnering

Appreciative Inquiry (Ai) is a team-building management model which was first outlined by David Cooperrider in 1987. Working on his PhD, he found what he considered life-centric factors contributing to the highly effective functioning of the Cleveland Clinic in Cleveland, Ohio. The clinic became the first large site where management had made a conscious decision to use inquiry as a focus on using life-giving factors as a basis for organizational management. Dr. Cooperrider identified that the clinic's success was based on a different organizational approach.

In this approach, The Cleveland Clinic's management focused on the possibilities of people resources available to the organization by identifying and leveraging the strength of its staff, clients and customers, instead of focusing on the same group's shortcomings.

In reviewing the clinic's organization and processes, Dr. Cooperrider saw what management was doing was ***different*** to traditional management problem-solving. He described it as an ***appreciation*** for a team's strengths and goals. He wrote the term "**Appreciative Inquiry**" as a footnote in a presentation describing "**emergent themes**" for the Board of Governors of the Cleveland Clinic. The report created such a powerfully positive message that the Board requested ways to disseminate and use this process within the entire group's practice.

Traditional management tries to identify and solve problems by addressing and bolstering weaknesses in staffing. Contrary to this approach, Appreciative Inquiry (Ai) doesn't address deficits or try to force staff to conform to the goals of the organization.

Ai takes a shared strength and vision approach. Utilizing Ai, a firm can discover the existing strengths within the workings of it staff, and can leverage that strength to make the teams more high-performing. As the name suggests, Appreciative Inquiry is a management approach that is based on appreciation and inquiry.

With Ai there is appreciation for what the team is already accomplishing, and inquiry to help the team accomplish more.

The focus on Inquiry is supported by asking the team a series of "discovery questions" to identify a unified mission. This discovery identifies the team's purpose into a mission and vision and goals of the larger organization.

There was a similar purpose to the Construction Project Partnering movement which also began in the early 1980's. Construction partnering was a common team integration and collaboration tool which utilized the identification and leveraging of shared team strengths in order to help a construction project's participants—the general contractor and his trade contractors, the design professionals and the project's owners or developers—create an opportunity to understand the shared excitement and fear each team brought separately into the project. It was an attempt to develop a shared sense of purpose with parties in a project dependent on each other, but not contracted to each other.

Architects are painfully aware of the litigation which accompanies the construction process. Partnering was developed to help level the construction playing field, by creating a safe environment where trust, cooperation and true collaboration could exist.

While there have been measures of attitude shift after project partnering--fewer claims, greater adherence to schedule--the successes of individual project partnering did not typically transcend the project and move upstream to the separate partner organizations. Indeed, design firms did not see the need to institute partnering throughout their projects as a typical management tool. In some cases, **partnering was promoted as a costly tool that masked and facilitated a contractor's deception.** We suggest that by adding Ai to Partnering, the design firm can change the temperament of a partnering session from an individual team bullying mission into a team-visioning process that creates mutual dreams and successes. Ai identifies a positive achievements approach, not just for the project but for each participating firm.

Ai changes the agenda from one of identifying and blaming--where the main mission is to expose the differences between all parties involved, and then force them to "play-nice"--to one of pinpointing positive results which have occurred in the past, and sharing stories and results that strengthen and inspire the participants. This activity facilitates the creation of shared project goals. The Ai process doesn't pretend that problems don't exist; it just approaches the problems from the other side- the side of identifying what IS working rather than what is NOT working. Once identified, the team can align to achieve the vision of shared strength they've created together.

In order to leverage Ai, the firm must build on several basic precepts:

1. In every project, organization and team there is a dynamic positive force to reach a successful goal.

2. What we focus on becomes our reality.

3. The formal act of asking questions to the team influences the direction of the team.

4. The team's and project success already exists.

Be the change you want to see in the world.

Ai is based on the assertion that project's "problems" are the results of the team's perspectives and interactions with perceptions of phenomena. For instance, if Ai recognizes a certain type of behavior as problematic, then the team's ability to effectively identify and address a group solution is constrained. Rather than trying to achieve a successful mission and vision, the group will focus on trying to fix the "problem".

Utilizing Ai inquiry techniques, the team visualizes as a group the best outcome of the project based on shared best conditions in the past. Using queries, the team identify and share what worked best for them in the past (identifying share strengths) and project those successes into the future, of what a successful project looks like and is.

While best practices for creating successful project partnering are numerous, instituting Ai into the partnering process adds an additional dimension that ensures shared success.

Success-based Queries

The first step in utilizing Ai the construction partnering process is identifying and employing successful project discussion questions. Ai builds its results on question topic choice. For construction project partnering, the questions should facilitate the process of building a successful project. Because integration and change begins to take place at the same time as inquiry, the inquiry should focus on what is working with the team (instead of what *not* is working), so that the team can identify existing strengths that need to be recognized and leveraged. In using AI, sometimes the simplest affirmative topic question evokes a change of thinking within the team. In most cases, the change is not what is expected.

Using Ai focuses affirmative language changes the way a project team and organization thinks and operates. Changing the way a team thinks changes the way a team works. Creating a shift in thinking begins with active Ai questioning. Using Ai to move beyond the traditional management problem-solving approach, the team is able to focus on what works, so it can do more of it.

Here are some Ai questions the partnering team can ask in order to help augment the partnering process:

"Where do you, as a team member, see the project next week?"

"How would you describe the project's accomplishments and successes to your family next year?"

"How do you measure success for this project? How would your company measure success for this project?"

There are many measures of success for the Ai-based organization. One is the involvement and commitment of its staff; another is the reputation of the firm. Another would be the openness to new human resource ideas and opportunities.

See www.beyondredlines.com for KPIs and forms for creating an Ai-based People team and organizational metrics.

Training within Industry –Project Staff Training

Training within Industry –Project Staff Training Program

Using Program from WWII to train Project Staff

Effectively training project staff and capturing and diffusing that training is difficult

within any firm.

Narrative.

I think that maybe the profession's apprentice-based model is outdated. There's

this great new book called <u>Drafting Culture</u>, which delineates the creation of the drafting

"bible" – "Architectural Graphic Standards" (by Charles George Ramsey and Harold

Reeve Sleeper). Ramsey was the architect and Sleeper was the draftsman, and "Graphic

Standards" was a thick book of detailed drawings which tried to compile "standards" –

standard details, standard language, standard outlines of how the tools of the

profession (its drawings), should be developed. Drafting Culture explores the cataloging

of the changes in the profession that this index created.

In 1932 when Graphic Standards was first published, architecture was

undergoing a transition from vocation to profession—it was moving from the

draftsman's craft (to be mastered through apprenticeship), to the architect's

academically based knowledge. This change brought about a concomitant rise in social

status. The past "drafting culture" gave way to significant post-WWII changes in design

and building practice.

The profession continues to go through a crafts versus academic transition. In all

but a few states, in order to be licensed, we must achieve a Masters Degree level of education, plus three years intern development post graduation. In school we enter into a design education environment that is art-based. After graduation we're then thrust into a work world that is business-based. We are told to apply our skills immediately to an assortment of tasks that straddle art and business. During that time we make vain attempts to accomplish complicated duties that have taken our project supervisors years to learn. When we immediately fail or only complete about half of the tasks correctly, we discover that this hit or miss training is also how the managers supervising us have also learned.

Learning from WWII America

A program known as "Training Within Industry" (TWI) was developed and used during World War II to successfully train thousands of inexperienced American workers. After the war, TWI went on to become a global training program which helped revive the economic forces of many war-torn countries, including Germany, England, and especially Japan. TWI helped enable these economies the opportunity to reinvent their industrial and manufacturing training programs.

Because of the success it achieved in Japan, the TWI program is referred as the **"Roots of Lean,"** in that it helped Toyota and its TWI-trained staff become one of the largest and most successful globally-based organizations.

What is TWI and how is it different from other training programs? Can the ideas and training program be effectively transferred to the craft/business world of architecture?

The original WWII TWI trainers built the program to quickly create a skilled workforce for soldier-depleted factories. The TWI training model was created on the need for industry to train labor on its own within a short timeframe. TWI focused on the using what it called the "**five needs knowledge model**" to identify organizational requirements:

1. *Knowledge of the work:* this is the information that makes one business or industry different from other businesses and industries.

2. *Knowledge of the work responsibilities*: these are the company's policies, regulations, rules, and organizational requirements –the extrinsic knowledge of the firm

3. *Skill in instructing:* TWI had to abbreviate the traditional apprenticeship period. To do this it provided processes to help supervisors quickly develop a well-trained workforce, resulting in the motto, "If the worker hasn't learned, the trainer hasn't taught"

4. *Skill in improving methods:* by requiring the organizations supervisors and managers to identify and list each work related task and steps, the trainer and learner are able to identify areas for improvement together

5. *Skill in leading:* this "needs" identification helped the trainer, who may be a manager or a past-trainee learn to improve his/her ability to work with staff.

TWI outlined its training on a three-part program of *job instruction, job methods, and job relations.* The philosophy of the program was based on "training within the industry or within the factory," that is, to train employees and supervisors directly within the industry or organization environment so the newly-trained staff can then train other members of the industry and organization.

For instance TWI used the example of an optical glass manufacturer in which a skilled optical glass grinder required three years of apprenticeship before he could successfully turn out an acceptable product. It turned out that apprenticeship in the glass industry, as well as most industries, considers three years of service to be the minimum length required for a successful apprenticeship. Indeed, architecture follows that three year requirement with its **intern development program (IDP)**.

With TWI, team members quickly learned the task at hand, and took complete ownership of training in difficult systems and processes. They went on to become mentors in the improvement of those processes and transferred that knowledge to other internal teams and projects, as well as outside stakeholders like the client, contractor and agency teams.

The original TWI program consisted of three parts:

-**Job Instruction,**

-**Job Methods, and**

-**Job Relations**

Since the program was developed for training craft-based skilled labor, TWI's focus was on creating a skilled manual labor based workforce. We adopted TWI training to focus on the understanding and completion of skilled tasks. We modified the three-part jobs program to focus on the criteria of -

-Task Instruction,

-Task Methods and Systems, and

-Task Improvement

Task Instruction stresses understanding and teaches how to breakdown responsibilities by identifying each tasks:

1) important steps,

2) key points, and

3) the reasons for the key points

(see www.beyondredlines.com for the Task Breakdown Sheet).

Training within Industry worked because it tasked managers of factories to identify and list each step of each seemingly impenetrable and complicated task within the plant. The Job Instruction sheet would then be used to individually train each inexperienced trainee. The undertaking of creating breakdown sheets for each task requires the trainer to think through each task's action, identify each task's steps and list the reasons for each step before even beginning to train a staff member in the task.

These activities helped organize the trainer's thought and focus on the reasons for the task. Once the tasks were broken down, the individual staff training consisted of four steps:

Step 1. **Preparation** – this step helps the learner begin to think activity, which aids in the comprehension of the new idea;

Step 2. **Presentation** – this step adds the new idea to the tasks already represented within the learner's mind;

Step 3. **Application** – this step helps train the learner begin to apply what was presented and to understand how to check results;

Step 4. **Testing** – this step tests the ability of the learner to apply the new task without assistance from the trainer.

In our project, we applied the **TWI Job Methods** program to focus on individual and system tasks as **Task Methods and Systems**. Our program identifies, categorizes and links the relationship of the organization's individual tasks to other tasks and systems within the organization. This allows individual tasks, delineated through the task instruction sheet, to be measured against other tasks within the project's requirement. For example, in our study, we utilized Task Methods with the Task Instruction sheet for capturing contactor RFIs (Requests for Information). When we modified drawings, the changes were identified and measured against the system requirements for creating change orders and for collecting information for creating quality metrics (see Task Methods and Systems Sheet).

We modified the last TWI program, **Job Relations**, which was the TWI system for helping workers and management understand and work with other, into **Task Improvement.**

Task Improvement became the *kaizen* (which is Japanese for "continuous improvement") of our TWI process. Toyota's system of Lean Production is a business model that achieves "more with less." *Kaizen* is a major tool of that model in that entails continuous review of existing steps and promotes active removal or improvement of steps within a process.

In our study, we used these systems of task instruction and task improvement to formally instruct our inexperienced architectural staff to understand and complete complicated tasks involving construction administration (CA) activities with our healthcare and hospital design and construction in California.

Hospital construction services in California involve working not only with multiple and varied customers and stakeholders including doctors, contractors and owners, but an entire state agency known as **OSHPD (Office of Statewide Health Planning and Development)**. OSHPD demands a strict compliance to specific document processes and protocols. Maintaining construction administration compliance with these requirements in addition to properly following the processes necessary for traditional CA services is difficult and complicated.

Traditionally, CA teams carry the office's **functional adhocracy** to the construction trailer. The CA team is typically built around one or several senior and experienced individuals, who pass down their tacit knowledge, support explicit organizational requirements and transfer knowledge of working on-site in active construction conditions. The knowledge diffusion of this "**single master with many helpers**" creates organizational training issues. Additionally, in current practice, most firms find that these **masters** no longer exist within their organization. Indeed, the ones that do exist, are stretched thin across the numerous projects under construction within the firm. In this situation, the staff that is available for CA tasks are usually inexperienced and untrained staff. This was a problem we faced on our hospital project. TWI was used to mitigate it.

By implementing our version of TWI, our site-based staff was instructed more quickly and productively. They became a meaningful part of creating and improving systems, and creating a transferable skillset.

{see www.beyondredlines.com for downloadable forms}

Tethered Millennials

Tethered Millennials

Narrative:

"There is no training in our company," the young intern architect from Riverside told me. "We bring the skills we've learned with us and hope for the best."

"The boomers and the older guys who run firm could care less about what we do, or how we do it. They're more worried about our IPods and instant-messaging and watching you-tube and fooling around on the internet. The project architects hate their jobs and the project managers are just glorified and older project architects who hate their jobs even more and they still don't know what they're doing.

My world sure doesn't match theirs. I've got $80,000 dollars in college debt, and they make us wait 3 months before they give us health insurance, which we still have to pay $200 a month for."

A project manager, from the same firm, overhearing the exchange, soon pulled me aside. "What's wrong with these kids?" she said, "They feel so entitled. They should just be glad they have jobs."

"When I got out of college in the early 1990s there were no jobs at all, most of my class mates went off to work somewhere else, but not in architecture."

She said this was her 5th job, and the one that she'd been at the longest (4 years), but the firm didn't care about training her, figuring she had learned all she needed at her past jobs. "Yeah right," she said, "what they want me to do now is get registered. They won't let me move up beyond Associate unless I'm licensed. But management got licensed *years ago before computers when it was just pencil and paper. They don't even know*

what the new test looks, or even how to study for it." She snorted, "some of the old

timers don't even know that you take the test with a computer now.."

Successfully staffing the architectural firm seems to be a complicated and never-ending process. For the employee it is even more of an adventure. A young designer's entry into the business of architecture has traditionally been gained by successfully climbing over numerous hurdles which are placed before her as she works her from school to designer to project architect and finally project manager. Sometimes those hurdles come from narrow expertise available within a single office. Sometimes, those hurdles are self-made as an employee jumps around from firm to firm, trying to find the right fit for her career.

From the firm-side, each year a firm faces different staffing needs and requirements. Sometimes these staffing issues sort themselves into generational groups, like the **Baby Boomers, GenXrs, or Millennials**. These generational groups are broadly stereotyped (often as a shortcut to aggregate ability or expertise). What is lacking in the relationship between the firm and the emerging professional is an overall best practice for young apprenticeship training, as well as the best way to groom managers and leaders. As most architecture firms are small firms, this challenge is greater because these firms are the firms that typically lack the money and talent resources to actually develop a staff training program.

Three chapters in this book focus on people-training issues. This chapter is a focus on a philosophical training approach to understanding how different generations work together within the workplace and client realm. The second reviews a WWII training program and outlines how it was used for the on-site team at a hospital construction project. The third chapter addresses the issues with utilizing a distribution workforce within the profession.

When this book was begun, the latest generation group entering the workplace, Millennials, was turning offices upside down in its attempt to accommodate them. The stories firms told of trying to deal with them were a regular feature at conferences. They were demanding and smug, convinced of their own abilities and

Tethered Millennials, Training the Net Generation –

Strauss and Howe in their book-_Generations (1991)_, proposed the theory of

generational progression, where every generation of twenty or so years, reacts to and is

part of the previous generation's systems and framework.

In 2000 they published _Millennials Rising_. This work investigated the emergence

of the Millennials, born 1982 to 2001, and their relationship with their previous

generations, the Boomers and Gen-X. They suggested that instead of the downbeat and

alienated students the Boomers and Gen-Xrs were when they were growing up,

Millennials would be different, they were already engaged and upbeat. The reasons for

this was what they described as their **"Generational Awakening Theory"**, which cast

Millennials as the "next great" generation, even comparing their potential to the last

great generation, that of the GI WWII vets.

In developing this theory, Strauss and Howe divided generations against the

peaks and valleys in cultural trends and history. According to their theory, there are

four repeating trends which create each generational group. These trends are: **Civic,**

Adaptive, Idealist and Reactive. **Civic** starts the generational trend with the **GI**

generation of WWII. The GIs were born between 1901-and 1924.

The **Adaptive** follows in the next generation, this time the **Silent Generation**,

taking their name from a Time Magazine article which described them as, "Youth

waiting for the hand of fate to fall on its shoulders, meanwhile working fairly hard and

saying almost nothing. The most startling fact about the younger generation is its silence. With some rare exceptions, youth is nowhere near the rostrum. By comparison with the Flaming Youth of their fathers & mothers, today's younger generation is a still, small flame. It does not issue manifestoes, make speeches or carry posters. It has been called the "**Silent Generation**". **Silents** were born between 1925 and 1942.

Baby Boomers follow, born between 1943 and 1960, and Strauss and Howe describe them as the Idealist group.

GenX follows as Reactive between 1961 and 1981. And Millennials then follow to repeat the Civic trend and are born between 1982 and 2001. See the chart below for each Strauss and Howe generational characteristics.

Generational Group	Trend	Birth Year	Characteristics
G.I. Generation	Civic	1901-1924	respond to a social crisis (WWII); focus on common good, Community, rebuilding the world
Silent	Adaptive	1925-1942	flexible; sensitive to diversity (told to stay out of the way, we're busy' during WW2). Note: no US president or UK prime minister from this group
Boomers	Idealist	1943-1960	spiritual awakening; aim to 'take things forward'
GenX	Reactive	1961-1981	cynical, pragmatic, questioning
Millennial	Civic	1982-2001	optimistic, success-oriented, conservative
New Silent	Adaptive	2001-2022	Similar to the silent?

According to this theory, Millennials are entering the workplace with a lot of promise. However, right now, the older generations view them as the tethered generation, continuing being raised into adulthood by their hovering parents long after they have finished college and entered the workforce. They are the single pet-children who were raised with not only seatbelts, but side airbags, baby monitors, bicycle helmets, scheduled playdates, and participation trophies. Because of this, they are viewed as wanting to be continually protected, entertained, scheduled, needing instant rewards, and expecting to run the firm (if not the world), by their second full week on the job.

Strauss and Howe write about how wonderful this new "Civic" workforce will be, however we, as executives and managers, must determine if we need to change the entire workplace to help them learn to work for us.

This challenge is compounded by the fact that there are four generations active in the workplace. We are now working with Silents, Baby Boomers, Xr's as well as these new Millennials. And we're doing it in within our combined organizational adhocracies.

Who are these generations and how can they work together in today's office?

Millennials and their promise and challenge

This chapter was written as a primer on Millennials; raised as over-scheduled children, they were nurtured with parent organized playdates. They have been taught to be experiential learners; preferring learning by doing, but within a framework of organization. They never read directions and prefer to learn by interacting with the technology, but also asking by questions to those who supposedly know more. They've grown up with multiplayer gaming, computer simulations, and social networks. These communities provide no penalty for this trial-and-error style of learning, so Millennials make mistakes, and have to learn how to properly "learn from their mistakes".

Watching Millennials interact with their phones and chats, we witness their nomadic communication style. They seem to be communicating with someone constantly through texting, chatting and cell phones wherever and whenever, mobile or fixed, work or play.

Millennials state that they are agnostic toward media and IT platform formats: Mac or PC, whatever, and they're still surprised that the rest of the wired isn't. They can learn and utilize interactive full motion, multimedia, graphical presentations, and audio in any format (as long as it's easy to post online). They are comfortable with moving these new technologies into the workplace as necessary (have them help you with your interview presentations).

Within their immediate families, because many are singletons, they respect adulthood and mature conversations. They strive to be learning, value intelligence and education. Most will have gone directly to graduate school after completing their undergraduate studies. This characteristic will make them the first generation in history where the majority of its members have multiple college degrees. But because of the college requirements, they also come into the workplace with excessive debt from student loans.

Millennials are collaborators. After many years of being taught to play nice during playdates, daycares, schools, and soccer teams, they now embrace peer-to peer networks, social-networking sites, and other structured team activities, Millennials know how and when to work with other people more effectively. Even those who do not prefer collaboration typically will try to collaborate, especially if they think it gives them a practical advantage.

Should a firm change to prepare for Millennials? The firm must measure outcome-based performance with formal balanced scorecard metrics. If the Millennials in your office are getting the job done faster than anticipated, then give them more to do. Don't settle for poor quality, but try not to get angry if they are also conducting personal conversations (or watching YouTube) while they're working.

Keep Millennials engaged (actually this should be true with everyone). "If my skills are developing, I'll stay here. If not, I'll go develop them somewhere else." Rotate Millennials through projects, mentor and reverse-mentor them with older staff, and formally help them with career planning and professional registration. Celebrate their achievements (remember the post soccer season pizza parties?), and help engage them for the next season.

Just as you should have done for your Boomers (long ago), and Xr's (more recently), your firm should offer your Millennials multiple mentors and scheduled help and registration for the Intern Development Program. Back in the early 1990's, Xr's came into the workforce during multiple recessions, and were expected to just be happy to have a job. Up until now (2008), Millennials had never experienced a recession, and expected the employer to be happy to have them working for you. They expect to be treated differently. Create a structure within the firm that encourages self-confidence and assuredness. Their parents told them "you can do it!" and so, they know they can (even if you know they can't). They come from a background that featured loving parents who scheduled their own lives around them. They will expect that same attention from you and your firm.

But what about these other generations still within the workplace; **The Silents, the Boomers, and the Xrs?** They will not be going away anytime soon. How should the firm work with this blended community of workers?

According to the Strauss and Howe Generational Awakening theory, each generational group plays its part as an actor in the span of time. **Millennials are the Civic generation (last seen with GIs)** that will focus their energy on the common good. They will try to do what's best for the organization, the community and world.

The **Adaptive** group follows the **Civic** and reacts neutrally against this civic goodness. The **Adaptives** stay out of the way and keep to themselves. Silents are the adaptive generation group that is with us today. **John McCain is a Silent**.

The **Idealist** group follow the **Adaptives.** Rather than being neutral, or focusing on the common good, **they tend to focus on themselves. Boomers are Idealists;** the current "me" generation.

Reactives follow **Idealists. Reactives** look at the wasted opportunities that the self-centered **Idealists** missed and become ironic and cynical. **Gen Xr's are our**

Reactives. They shake their heads at the Boomers and wonder what happened. As for

ironic and cynical, one need only look at the comedy of Jon Stewart and Chris Rock to

see the GenXr view of past generations.

In understanding how each generation views the workplace, we need to see

them through the same lens we've focused on **Millennials**.

Silents. This is the Korean War vet generation. Born from 1925-to 1942, they

were in their 20's and 30's in the 1950's just in time for nuclear and cold wars. If

Millennials were molded by 9-11, **Silents** were molded by their older sibling's role in

WWII and the Soviet Blockades and Iron Curtains that followed. In this group, only males

were in the workforce, women stayed at home and raised families (94%).

Only 22% went to college and the 1950/60's work was in major industries (70%

currently have some sort of pension plan (ask your Millennials if they even know what a

pension plan is)). In the 1950/60's, this group had full health insurance, vacation and

sick plans, and company cars. What they didn't have was a safe world. In 1952, at the

end of a particular nasty epidemic, 58,000 people had been infected with Polio resulting

in over 3,000 deaths. Life expectancy was 65 years for men, 70 for women. Minorities

and women didn't exist in the workforce (at least in their workforce), and most

everyone working in the US was from a European background.

Times make the man. In 2009, this group is now in its late 60's to 80's. They're

working because they still can. They've helped bring about great changes in the workplace. They've moved from a workplace of working only with each other (as white guys) to a workplace that is half minorities and women. However, they still have their workplace requirements that they have beat into their Boomer and Gen-Xer workforce. 8 hour (minimum, all at the same time) workdays, office and personal time don't mix (remember, they had someone at home to run the household errands), and the expectation that staff should be happy if not grateful for having a job, and being able to do any type of work.

A lot of the resentment to young staff's seemingly inordinate behavior and demands comes from the background of its leaders.

Baby Boomers.

Remember these are Idealists, and are currently driving our adhocracies. This huge cohort, born 1943 to 1960 practically runs everything right now. In 2009, we've lived life under Boomer control since the late 1980s. However, before running things their defining moments included Woodstock (of course), Vietnam, the Birth Control Pill, and Nixon's Resignation.

The business world works to support Boomers ideology. However, during the Boomers management, things haven't improved across the board. During Boomers time at the wheel, health care costs have rocketed, personal savings has decreased from 12% in 1982 to 2.5% in 2008. And the current economic mess can be blamed on their lack of forward looking oversight.

GenX.

This cohort was born from 1961-1981. These workers followed the Boomers into the workforce and were quickly met with a one-two punch of inflation and recession. Interest rates were 19% during President Reagan's first term in 1981. Then there was the savings and loan crisis right after, in the mid-1980's, there was the mini-stock market crash in 1986, and then rolling regional recessions that rocked the profession through the early 90s. I attended the AIA national convention in 1990 in DC and the majority of the sessions were on alternate (non-architect) careers.

In addition to the economy, X'rs defining moments were the Challenger Space Shuttle explosion, the Berlin Wall and Soviet collapse, and the first Gulf war. Xr icons were **Less than Zero and Kurt Cobain and Alf** (and He-man and Skeletor). Xrs came into age in the 1980s and then wondered what was happened in the 1990s, until the end of the 90's when some of them made big money with the internet.

When we discuss these ideas, we need to measure their impact against the background of -

Recency, Infrequency, Out-Group, and Adolescent Illusions -

Recency Illusion is the belief that public observations are in fact just *recent*. Each old generation experiences a "these kids today" moment with each new generation. For example, I remember my father (who is a Silent), vociferously complaining about the work ethic of the Boomers back in the 1960s and 70s. Remind yourself of the Vietnam War protests

Infrequency Illusion is the belief that a feature the public has just noticed is rarer and more notable than it really is. If something feels new to us then it must be new to everybody else too. There is a natural tendency to overestimate our own personal experience and not step back and look at the big picture. Wow, you mean these kids refuse to do that? And no one is telling them no? We'd never get away with that when we were their age.

The Out-Group Illusion is the tendency to blame undesirable trends on some other group of people. It's them not us. Millennials are causing the problems because they expect special training.

The corollary to the Out-Group is the **Adolescent Illusion**. This is the blaming of current bad events on the younger generation.

With staff training we should remember that we should properly assess skills that each worker brings to the workplace, make sure they have the proper tools (software, computers, etc), and then ensure that they are properly trained and that their skills are adequately updated. With Balanced Scorecard metrics focusing on People processes, a firm can build an annual database that ensures properly updated training.

Layoffs

The new challenge with Millennials is the challenge of the new depression. While the firm tolerated the quirks of their needs and personalities over the last five years, now Millennials are becoming the new unemployed generation. Gen-X and Boomers battled their own bouts of unemployment in the 1970's 80's and 90's, but we thought that globalization had created a permanent wave of prosperity. As the events of the last years are forcing more staff onto the street, how should we best help the youtube generation to stay connected in the profession and in their career?

1) Remind them that it's not a job but a career. A career has many facets and functions. There are different ways to get experience with or without firms. Help them use their social-networking skills to do small projects outside of the office with other former co-workers. Help them get copies of autocad, revit, and other modeling and drafting software, so that they can continue learning and training.

2) Continue to support their IDP processes. If you can no longer pay an "employee", you can still be a mentor to their development, and support their IDP processes. Now is the time to help them through the difficult to complete sections of IDP. And while you may be overstretched and distracted with your firms response to this depression, helping a former employee continue to work through their IDP will help keep them in the profession. (Check NCARB requirements for "employee" status issues.

3) Offer financial advice. While dumping and forgetting about an employee is the easiest thing to do, suggest that they stay in contact with the project managers and architects. Offering pipeline assistance such as project knowledge dissemination, client calls, and project filing will help stabilize the firm. It will also show that you have systems in place that support training and service. Helping your former employee will also provide good role-model services and help them learn not to burn bridges.

While these are difficult times, they won't last forever. Your former employees will soon be competing with you for work. They will have learned your best and worst processes, they will know your firms flaws and strengths, and they will soon surpass you in their abilities. Treating a valuable member of your team as if they were still a valuable member will be an investment that will payoff as they invite you to bid with them on a future joint venture, or suggest your firm's name for that addition, or smile at you from the front row of the selection committee. And if all you can remember is that you took that "kid's ipod away" or made her "remove her chat account from the office laptop" (even though she said she was using it to real-time chat with the field team about coordination issues), then you'll have a hard time smiling back.

Ensuring Quality Performance with a Distributed Workforce

Ensuring Quality Performance with a Distributed Workforce

In the need to go global, firms are asking their employees to be effective across distances never before mastered, depending on new innovations in communication to tie everyone together.

This chapter will outline not the hard technological tools, not the servers, not the ftp sites, or the cloud computing, but the **soft human tools like communication and chat and record keeping** that a firm should utilize for remote offices, field staff, traveling executives, and well as contingent workforce and outsourcing.

Narrative: How does a firm utilize outsourcing, contractors, or even crowdsourcing? How does the firm deal with executives on the road, staff stationed at jobsites, multiple offices. Additionally, most industries have found ways to utilize workers from all over the world, but my office is content with complaining about the abilities of our current staff instead of considering how to work with a distributed staff. There may be experienced staff that the firm could use in India, the Philippines, North Dakota, or even one of our other offices. How can management take advantage of technology that links everyone to everyone else while still ensuring the local staff feels involved?

Singing songs in their native tongue.

Trust and Control with Presence Awareness.

We work with distributed project teams that are located within the same office as well as 50 and 1,000 miles away, and around the world. In order to work successfully with these team members we have to use a combination of Trust, Control and Presence Awareness.

Trust is defined as the confidence and willingness to rely on another party under conditions of risk or vulnerability.

Control is the ability to influence actions of others.

Presence awareness is one group's awareness of other people or groups being available to them online. Presence awareness is the sense of "being around and available."

We establish formal project engagements for our teams in order engage our teams in order to establish trust close and at a distance. This begins with-

1) –Formal Socialization.

2) –Transparent communication and formal record keeping.

3) –Presence awareness –emails, texting, chat and nightly skyping

4) –Creation of a balance between central control and local discretion.

By identifying and developing formal trust and control procedures, we are able to establish a strong **"presence awareness"** within the organization. For example, when a teacher leaves a classroom, the students react according to their awareness of where that teacher might be. If she's right outside the door, they'll act differently than if she has left the building. For a workforce thousands of miles away, the team's presence awareness is a necessary requirement to keep working.

Presence awareness confers a sense of immediacy and intimacy, along with a projecting the firm's social culture requirements. *Immediacy* in business communication is presented through actions such as nodding or smiling, demonstrating a reflection of immediate comprehension and understanding. *Intimacy* in a business environment is experienced by verbal and non-verbal behavior, indicating familiarity and closeness. Intimate behavior is subconscious and maintained in equilibrium by the interactors during the communication process.

Picture two people flirting at a bar.

Immediacy and intimacy are easy to convey in face to face (F2F) interaction, but in a remote, or tele-presence (telephone, teleconference, email and chat) medium, the correct generation of these behaviors can become difficult.

One of my favorite stories involves me trying to sell tomatillos to Naomi, (an old-order Amish woman) by telephone. I was living in Philadelphia, and I had a surplus quantity of organic tomatillos from my backyard garden that she had agreed to purchase. I had sold an initial quantity to her directly at Reading Terminal Market. She

said that she expected to sell-out that quantity and wanted me to call her to determine

how many more she needed. Call you?, I asked, knowing that she was Amish and

wouldn't normally have a phone available (this was long before cell phones, which are

currently disrupting the Amish community, but that's another story). She said, just call

Tony at the Italian Market stall next to hers, he'll come over and get me.

So I had a bunch of beautiful tomatillos, I called Tony and asked if he could ask

Naomi to come and take my call. She answered the phone, saying hello. I said hello in

reply and asked how she was. "I'm fine, thank you," she said. I then asked her if she

would like some of my tomatillos.

Silence.

Naomi, I asked, are you still there?

Silence.

Naomi? Can you say yes if you're still there.

"Yes, she replied"

"I have about 10 pounds of tomatillos, would like me to bring them down to

you?"

Silence.

I was wondering what was happening. The connection was still good, as I could

still hear the noise of the market in the background. "Wait a minute," I thought.

"Naomi, I said, are you nodding your head? Could you please answer yes or no?"

"Yes," she said, "I'm nodding my head. Yes, please bring them down."

"I'll be down within an hour. Is that okay?" I asked.

Silence.

"Are you nodding yes?" I asked, "Will an hour work for you?"

"Yes" she said.

The nodding and not talking was a lesson she had not learned about telephone etiquette. Rather than saying uh-huh, and yes, and okay, and that sounds good, she only occupied the face to face (F2F) realm with nodding and eye contact. This is how we as a profession are still learning to use chat and email, nodding when we should be talking, and waiting for eye contact when the other team cannot see us.

Intimacy and Immediacy

In order for an organization to create and successfully manage presence awareness within its distributed network, it should plan to formally move beyond traditional communicators such as telephones, conference calls and email. Lacking intimacy and immediacy telephones and email cannot offer the subtle status checks and presence awareness that must become a part of a successful distributed workforce. While some firms struggle with higher resolution video conferencing technology, or co-located teams, there is a far simpler tool that is available for free to any employee with a computer and an internet connection. That tool is - **Chat**.

Chat works with a distributed team by establishing the immediate awareness of the availability of a communication partner. Based on legacy familiarity, most architects think that, in lieu of direct face to face **(F2F)** communication, telephones provide a better vehicle for constant contact. While this may be true for the single point or arbitrary contact that comes with planned client or vendor communication, chat actually provides a better vehicle for the regular and deep communication required between coworkers or team members.

Chat accomplishes this by utilizing the factors of immediacy and intimacy. With chat or texting, immediacy is achieved by showing presence awareness in the background "I know you're around and available, and that you will respond when I need you". Intimacy in chat is achieved by utilizing shorthand U's instead of You and 8's to fill in h8 and sk8, and, with some programs, "emoticons," those smiley-faces, or dancing stick people that are used to add dimension to the margins of chat.

Because of this **Chat** offers a richer presence awareness than a telephone call or an email. Chat allows coworkers to maintain connection with others outside the context of specific events of information exchange. Chat creates a connectedness through immediacy.

These **immediacy** behaviors are defined by:

1) co-presence, co-location and mutual awareness. These factors express the elements of being together;

2) creating the experience of psychological involvement, including saliency and making oneself known; and

3) establishing behavioral engagement, by focusing each team member to communicate within the context of the requirement which creates social presence.

Chatting is communication in which the sender and receiver share a common, though asynchronous, experience. Sending a message refreshes the contact between the two people or group. Social presence is the perception of another participant as well as the medium itself. Connectedness is creates an emotional experience, caused by the other participant's presence.

Chat creates presence awareness while allowing the team to negotiate interruptions. Chat works with around the world staff, near distributed staff, within the building staff, sitting next to each other staff. For next door staff, chat works better than telephone calls and in-person conversations which are among the most common sources of interruption. (there are also the calls checking on receipt of email; "Hi, did you get my email?").

Co-workers who are aware of the person they need to interrupt to communicate with, will initiate these interactions in order to avoid disruptions, listening and waiting until they hear a free space around the individual they need to talk to. Chat provides a tool to negotiate these interactions.

From the sender's point of view, chat becomes an unobtrusive way to test availability. Although a chat pop-up is disruptive, it is not as distracting as an unplanned telephone call or an unexpected office visit.

From the recipient's point of view, chat provides two techniques for managing availability. **First,** unlike a telephone, **chat flags its availability**, minimizing unwanted interruptions. The co-worker may request to postpone the conversation. **Secondly**, it's also **acceptable to ignore** an incoming text when a person is away from the computer. Chat provides a means of obtaining task relevant information rapidly and with minimal disruption, allowing a teammate to ask clarifying questions without the expectation of engaging in a longer conversation. It can also be used to participate in a sustained form of low-intensity collaboration.

Communicating via chat is easier than making a phone call, and the line can be kept open indefinitely, allowing participants to ask each other infrequently with the expectation that a response will be forthcoming. However, chat enables workers to handle their work/life balance less disruptively. Non-work chat communications can be integrated seamlessly into the work environment, allowing quick, conveniently timed check-ins with family and friends without requiring relatively longer periods of off-task time that the telephone requires.

Chat also allows more frequent and briefer use of such media as email, telephone, and face-to-face interactions. According to research, 72% of chat report that they communicate with coworkers online every day or several times a day. Similarly, 44% of chat users communicate this frequently via the computer with clients, compared to only 34% of non-users.

With chat, personal communications are not time consuming: **Telephone interruptions demand immediate attention** (the phone rings until answered or until the call goes to voice mail), can be difficult to reschedule (think phone tag), and tend to be longer in duration. Chat facilitates control over the timing, frequency, and duration of communication.

In this context, chat results in reduced workplace interruption. However, just like staff using other technologies, formally implementing chat into a team makes the tool available for their own communication goals, styles of interaction, and modes of use. The same attributes of chat that create new opportunities for workplace interruption also enable its users to manage interruption more effectively. **Twitter** is a form of **group Chat**. Twitter offers a group of people your presence awareness.

Video Conferencing doesn't work.

If chat works so well, how about video-conferencing, that's got to work even better, right? Although chat is *not* a substitute for F2F communication in terms of providing a sense of connection, with the factors of immediacy and intimacy, Chat is actually more intimate than video-conferencing. Video is a poor substitute for high-fidelity F2F interactivity. Even though it attempts to **create the social benefits of shared common physical space**, it usually ends up as a distracting mess of low bandwidth dropouts and latency issues. Video conferencing lacks the intimacy of chat. WebTV by Microsoft never caught on, because who wanted everyone in the room to read your emails on TV. With video conferencing, side conversations are unintentionally broadcast, the team feels like they're in an episode of TMZ and can't scratch their nose, or adjust their underwear without everyone watching. In most cases, the technology of Video Conferencing overwhelms the requirements of the conference.

Avatar Conference Space

There are virtual group chats that are beginning to make headway into the business environment. These are Second Life type spaces with avatars that act on behest of the chat attendees. In the case of a particular project, the project team could build a project website where team members could come to meet and check out files, download the latest project information, and update the team with progress. **Lively by Google**, allows users to create private rooms and chat avatars for conferences. **Qwaq** is the first business centric virtual world creator that offers a robust group chat conference facility. However, these **second life worlds lack the immediacy**, and will most likely work better as visually interactive sharepoint sites, containing the inventory of a project in easy to access folders, while the team chats in the background.

Cultural boundaries

In our experience with working with remote teams, the more remote the partner, the more likely cultural boundaries will be conflicted and crossed, with all its concomitant effects on trust and control, immediacy and intimacy, and common ground and practice. There are two important factors that make it difficult for culturally remote distributed teams to engage in productive worksharing commitments-

1. **Lack of common social identity** –the team is unaware of the environment the other team is a part of..

2. **Increased compositional diversity** –the hierarchies and roles the distributed team contains in its work flows and communication..

A firm creating a successful distributed team understands how important it is to implement mediated communication in order to create immediacy and intimacy. In developing worksharing and distribution, it is important to understand the topology, the shape, feel, and comprehension, of the mediated communication. Effective mediated communication should have components of:

1. **Audibility** –Participants hear other people and sounds in the environment around the participant

2. **Visibility** –Participants see other people and objects in the environment

3. **Tangibility** –Participants can touch other people and objects in the environment

4. **Co-presence** –Participants are mutually aware that they share a physical

environment

5. **Mobility** –People can move around in a shared environment

6. **Co-temporality** –Participants are in the same place at the same time

7. **Simultaneity** –Participants can send and receive messages at the same time.

8. **Sequentiality** –Participants take turns, and one turn's relevance to another is signaled by adjacency.

9. **Reviewabliliy** –Messages do not fade over time but can be reviewed.

10. **Revisability** –messages can be revised before being sent.

If these affordances are not completely available, then the distributed team must make up the difference with the affordances that are available. Utilizing these active affordances, the team needs to move quickly to repair misunderstanding within communications which are usually demonstrated as:

1. Misunderstandings in communications and

2. Strangely escalating conflicts.

Without utilizing chat, email follow up to telephone conversation can develop fragmented gaps and misunderstandings. For example

-confusion in telephone conference calls, people on different pages of documents during the call,

-group members failing to return phone calls.

-leaders and project managers surprised by unexpected reactions to their decision from distant sites.

-some resulted in resisting reason and ended up played a role in self-perpetuating feuds.

US and THEM.
In our project, we found that:

1) managers had **difficulty transferring cultural subtleties** (how we do things around here) across cultural dimensions;

2) **distance blocked corrective feedback** that is provided by chance encounters outside of the team tasks. Team members often run into each other during non-team events. Misunderstanding builds up between distant teams that could not enjoy casual opportunities that close proximity offers;

3) Once a team or individual team member was **out of sight** (off skype, or not within a presence awareness) she was **out of mind**

4) **Short is long** –even if the team is separated by a floor (if proximity is somewhere else, it doesn't matter where it is), the absence of proximity turns a close team member into a distant member

5) **Time is distance**. When working with asynchronous distributed teams (India as well as edge time zones within the United States), it is important to know that time creates distant. We have a team member in ET (3 hours ahead of our PT), who is always scheduling conference calls at 10am his time (7am our time). We get back by scheduling our calls at 4pm our time (7pm his time).

6) **Influence of changes between the home office and periphery**. For example, we noted a team member who quickly became a different person when he went to the remote supplier. Smaller firms are more vulnerable to this in that their limited staffs had been hired for one tech purpose;

7) **Promote Integration practices** that span distances and time differences

F2F

When a team has an opportunity for F2F meetings, they should focus on using that time to build commitment to the project and firm's purpose. A goal of the balanced approach should be to practice developing an accurate shared awareness of the team and firm's missions and goals as a unifying exercise during F2F's.

Shared understanding and commitment is required when working across distances. It's recommended that remote leaders that are nearer to each other should try to meet F2F every 8 weeks. In these near teams, they should try to vary each other's sites, and have formal telephone conferences every 3 weeks, personal calls weekly, chats daily.

Utilizing shared humor and jokes as one type of socializing tools can help delineate the importance in guiding all group members in articulating and embodying group norms, roles and procedures in working and communicating together. Effective leaders convene and facilitate repeated group discussion of issues. The team begins to understand subtle guidance requirements, as instead of asking another distance team member to complete a task, a firm delivery date is required, such as: "I need you to review these items by (your) next Monday."

Encourage Presence Awareness

Presence awareness in creating personal relations can help bridge distance issues in distributed work. Some final observations include-

1. **Encourage layered communications** -while chat should be the standard, the team shouldn't completely abandon email and telephonic voice communication, as well as continuing to utilize teleconference and video conferencing groupware

software.

2. **Don't use remote sites as a way to punish leaders** who may have peripheralized themselves while at HQ (through clashes in style, fundamental disagreements, or rebellious relations). Their presence made the remote sites feel more remote.

3. Distance among members of a **distributed work group is multidimensional**, there are time, culture as well as distance issues.

4. The impact of distance on the performance of a distributed **workgroup is not directly proportional to objective measure of distance.** In other words, you may have some of your best experiences with the more remotely separated teams

5. The difference in the effects that distance have on work groups are due to 2 sets of integrating practices- **practices that help members effectively span distances** and **an organizational context and structure that support the group** as its members work across distance.

The final discussion for distributed teams are issues regarding Conflict and Resolution.

Conflict and Resolution

Conflict and the necessary resolution is fundamental to any successful group functioning. Conflict is based on two issues – Relationship based or Task Related based.

Relationship conflict is an awareness of interpersonal incompatibilities that have occurred between teammates. Examples include hurt feelings about way a team mate has acted toward another team mate.

Task conflict is an awareness of difference in viewpoints and opinions pertaining to the group's task. Examples are disagreements among group members ideas about the task being performed, disagreement regarding hiring practices, or what to include in the annual report.

As one would guess, perceptions of task and relationship conflict are highly correlated. **Misattribution,** or mistaking a task-focused comment as a personal attack are examples of task and relationship overlap.

This is becomes more important when teams are new and just beginning to work together. We're all aware of Bruce Tuckman's Teaming phases of "**Forming, Storming, Norming, Performing**" cycle, which states that these are required phases for the team to grow, identify and face challenges, to tackle problems, and to find solutions, and to deliver.

To move through these phases with maturity and growth, the team must first establish trust. Trust requires a different set of behaviors. Trust helps people avoid interpreting conflict as relationship-based even when task conflict is heightened.

Forming, Storming, Norming, Performing
Forming

In the first stages of team building, the team forming takes place. During this phase the team meets and learns about the project's milestones, delivery schedule, and opportunity and challenges. They also agree on goals and responsibilities. During this first phase, team members still act independently to other team members. As members of previous project teams, they are excited and motivated but are still relatively uninformed of the issues and objectives of the team. During Forming, team members are on their best behavior but still focused on themselves. The project manager and other experienced and mature team members should begin to demonstrate model appropriate behavior even at this early phase.

The forming phase is where the members of the team get to know one another and make new friends. Each team member is watching how other members of the team works, takes or gives commands and see how each respond to pressure and stress.

Storming

The next phase is storming. In storming, team members form alliances and conflicts. The way tasks are identified and completed as well as what problems they are really supposed to solve, how they will function independently and together and what leadership model they will accept. Remember adhocracies run the organization. During storming, team members open up to each other and confront each other's ideas and perspectives, and establish **their role within the adhocracy**.

Management should try to help teams **move through the storming phase as quickly as possible**. In others, the team never leaves this stage. The maturity of some team members usually determines whether the team will ever move out of this stage. Some team members will focus on minutiae to evade real issues.

The storming stage is necessary to the growth of the team. It can be contentious, unpleasant and even painful to members of the team who are averse to conflict. Tolerance of each team member and their differences needs to be emphasized. Without tolerance, patience, and learning the team will fail. Without care, this phase can become destructive to the team and will lower motivation if allowed to get out of control.

During this phase, the teams' project managers should be accessible but need to be directive in their guidance of decision-making and professional behavior.

Norming

After Storming, the team enters the norming phase. Team members during this phase should adjust their behavior to each other as they learn and develop new work habits that make teamwork seem more natural and fluid. Team members often work through this stage by agreeing on rules, values, professional behavior, shared methods, working tools, acceptable jokes, pranks and even taboos. During this phase, team members begin to trust each other, and understand how each team member work. **Motivation increases as the team gets more acquainted themselves** and with the project.

Teams in this phase may lose their creativity if the norming behaviors become too strong and begin to stifle healthy dissent and the team begins to exhibit groupthink.

Supervisors of the team during this phase tend to be participative more than in the earlier stages. The team members can be expected to take more responsibility for making decisions and for their professional behavior.

Performing

The final phase for all successful teams is the performing stage. These high-performing teams are able to function as a unit as they find ways to get the job done smoothly and effectively without inappropriate conflict or the need for extra external management or supervision. At this phase, team members have become interdependent and effective. They are motivated and knowledgeable about who does what and how the work is getting done. The team members are now competent, autonomous and able to handle the decision-making process without supervision. Dissent is expected and allowed as long as it is channeled through means acceptable through the team.

Managers during this phase should be participative but hands off The team itself will make all of the necessary decisions.

However, even the most high-performing teams may revert to the earlier stages of forming and storming in certain circumstances if the project's requirements change. Indeed, many long-standing teams will go back through these cycles many times as they react to changing circumstances. For example, a change in team leadership may cause the team to revert to storming as the new people challenge the existing norms and dynamics of the team.

Onshore and Offshore teams

The Forming Storming Norming Performing cycle is harder to control with a remote team. The team will get bogged down within the storming behavior which can result in misunderstandings in communications and strangely escalating conflicts and self-perpetuating feuds. Distance hampers the corrective feedback that change encounters encourage.

Follow-the-sun methodology and Results Oriented Work (ROW)

Final aspect in working with a distributed team is how to deal with shifted time schedules. Our remote team experience dealt with teams located in India, in India Standard time which is 11.5 to 12.5 hours ahead of our Pacific Time zone (depending on daylight or standard time), we experimented with **Results Oriented Work** (ROW) timeshifts to ensure successful task completion. To mitigate our team from operating 24 hours 7 days a week, we worked to formally shape non-work time into our onshore team's workweek.

We started by implementing a 10am to 2pm core work time in which the team showed intentional presence awareness: either in the office or hard-logged and available on skype. The in-office or skype log-in becomes the time for the various on-shore (within a 3 hour time zone) internal teams to collaborate. The time before core time (6am to 10am) or after core time (2pm to 6pm), becomes time to work with client issues. The 10pm to 12midnight time is the skype offshore chat communication time.

With ROW our project managers communicate with the offshore team about their project's requirements from 10pm to 12mid Sunday night to Friday night (if the off-shore team works Saturday). ROW also establishes rules about availability and contact times. Nights between 12mid and 6am (PT) are blackout times (modified accordingly for non PT western hemisphere workers).

In closing, Presence Awareness Distributed Teams and ROW can help develop successful teams within your projects. See www.beyondredlines.com for forms and metrics for balanced management measures.

Bioteaming

Biomimicry is the science that studies the models, systems, elements and processes of nature, and then imitates or takes creative inspiration from them to solve human problems. Biomimicry has created Velcro, Michael Phelps' Fastskin, sharkskin swimming suit, and buildings that convect air similar to termite mounds.

Bioteaming is based on mimicking the groups in nature; from geese, to bees, to jellyfish, and then applying their concepts to human-based organizations. Bioteaming is not about humans trying to behave like ants or bees – but an examination of how to incorporate 10-million years of natural principles, to help make smart human teams more effective.

A bioteam utilizes

1) Collective Leadership: Any group member can take the lead. Nature's groups are never led exclusively by one member; different group members lead as needed.

2) Instant Messaging: Instant whole-group broadcast communications. Nature's teams use short instant messages that are instantly broadcast and received wherever the members are

3) Develop an ecosystem: Mass collaboration- from Wikipedia to Skype, *here comes everybody*, means that every team member shares resources and expertise.

4) Clustering: Engaging the many through the few. Trust the team, shared failure and rewards, incremental evolving improvement and clear

accountability.

5) Action-based: Each team member communicates three-dimensionally. – autonomously with each other, their environment, and with the organization

6) Self Management: Each team member manages itself and does not need to be told what to do.

A bioteam is not a leaderless team, but instead, a multi-leadered team. When there is a *why* either through a all-encompassing project mission statement, or a single project deliverable, the *why* leads the individual members of the team into group self-direction, with all members pitching in and helping create the direction and deliverables.

A bioteam is the evolved distributed workforce. Utilizing chat for short directional messages, implementing direction by

Technology adoption: the investment needed to learn the technology greatly exceeds the potential benefits

Accountability issues: teams find it much easier to break virtual commitments than verbal ones

Team mobilization: technology does not address the need for mobilizing action. It forces teams to use new tools without having first asked the proper strategic questions: who am I, where am I going, why do I want to get there?

New Working Practices: novel and unfamiliar working practices are just too difficult to adopt within a short amount of time

Overfocus on Technology and Process: not enough focus on production of results the dynamic and living nature of the team itself as a separate entity from that of its individual members.

A networked business team is a living entity in and of itself. A Virtual Networked Team is more than the sum of its member's abilities.

Traditional organizations treat teams mechanistically; thinking of teams as engines that are assigned to complete specific tasks and assignments. Traditional command and control management structures want the highest control and predictable work behavior. This is exactly the opposite of what nature's bioteams do.

The bioteam interpretation is that the team is a whole, living entity, which frames a more insightful interpretation of the most efficient courses of team action.

Ken Thompson and Robin Good in their brochure The Bioteaming Manifesto (2008) describes a successful bioteam as one that functions on principles-

1: Clear, transparent and public accountability

Successful bioteam members believe that every member of the team has a clear and public accountability. Every team member knows what she/he is responsible for and what she/he can count on the others for.

2. Trusted Competency

Bioteam members believe that the rest of the team trusts them to know how to do their job properly without being supervised. In a multidisciplinary team this translates into "I know what you have to do and am confident you can do it — how you do it is your business."

3: Give and Take

Bioteam members believe that if they need help they can ask for it and it will be freely offered. They believe that asking for help, with moderation, actually increases their standing within the team rather than diminishing it. They also believe something is wrong if somebody is struggling along and not asking for help or is asking for help but being ignored by the rest of the team.

4: Total Transparency

Bioteam members expect to be kept appraised in an honest and timely manner of any important issues in the project even if the issue does not directly affect them. This is part of the fore becoming capable of contributions beyond the ones normally dictated by their specific team role. Bioteam members also believe that individual team members should be free to pass opinions about situations they are not directly responsible for and that these opinions should always be highly respected and listened to.

5. Shared Glory

Bioteam members believe they are all in it together and that glory and pain will be shared. Like the four musketeers it is "One for all and all for one". HPT team members do not believe that their leader will take an unfairly big portion of the credit for a success or all of the blame for a failure. Underpinning this is the belief that each team member is equally accountable to the leader and fellow team members.

6: Meaningful Mission Value

Bioteam members believe that the group's operational mission is significant, important and meaningful. They believe that if they are successful they will have made a fundamental contribution to their organization and possibly to the greater good. If they saw the project as just 'business as usual' or routine, then their motivation would sag significantly. To foster this sentiment, the task must not seem trivial or easy or as if it has been done before. A bioteam also generally feel they are the only people in the organization who could succeed at accomplishing such a difficult task.

7: Outcome Optimism

Finally, as discussed under "Learned Optimism" bioteam members are confident that they (and they alone) will succeed in delivering the mission of the project.

They also recommend rules for creating a successful bioteam –

1. Stop Controlling; communicated information, not orders.

2. Utilize team intelligence; mobilize everyone on the team to look for and manage team threats and opportunities.

3. Permission granted; Achieve accountability through transparency not permission

4. Always-On; provide 24x7 instant messaging for all team members.

5. Symbiosis; treat external partners as fully trusted team members

6. Cluster; nurture the team's internal and external networks and connections.

7. Swarm; develop consistent autonomous team member behaviors.

8. Tit-for-Tat; Team members must learn effective biological and interpersonal cooperation strategies

9. Genetic Algorithms; Learn through experimentation, mutation, and team review

10. Self-Organizing Networks; Define the team in terms of 'network transformations' not outputs

11. Porous Membranes; Develop team boundaries which are open to energy but closed to waste (self-selecting teams)

12. Emerge; scale naturally through nature's universal growth and decay cycles.

A bioteam is seen as the evolution of work distribution through the global network. While teams and organizations have existed in small, local and regional organizations, the global interconnectivity of the world and cross-border social networking has established incredible opportunities for operational scaling.

See www.beyondredlines.com for KPIs, forms, and balanced spreadsheets for working

with a distributed workforce:

PROCESSES

PROCESSES

Processes

Everything a firm does involves a process.

While instituting **People** perspective scorecard requirements, the firm should also begin a formal review of its processes. This review is as important during troubled times as well as good because it starts an appraisal of how work flows through the office while cataloging the firm's institutional knowledge. Completing and publishing such reviews within a balanced scorecard framework identifies which processes can be modified or removed, as well as creating a framework for developing future processes with sustainable metrics.

A process review provides an opportunity for formal self-examination. The paradigm in which the architectural firm functions is constantly changing, shifting with each project's requirements. What was once a craft-based profession built on finely delineated hand-drawing is now a profession immersed in digital technology and digital delivery methods. **Adhocractic project-based organizations** face obstacles which must be overcome in order to capture and disseminate knowledge that is obtained from the relatively self-contained, idiosyncratic and finite nature of project tasks.

Utilizing balanced management, the Process Perspective provides a different insight into reviewing the existing process, protocols, and methodologies the firm utilizes in order to complete its work. This means reviewing the business processes within each perspective to see how they support the other perspectives. In the case of the process perspective, the firm would ask:

-Are the people perspective goals being hampered because the paperwork process requirements for staff training are too restrictive?

-Are the accounting department's invoicing processes creating additional work for project managers in terms of disputed collections?

-Are the business development processes hampering the acquisition of productive and meaningful clients?

Successful management is difficult for a firm if a number of unconnected processes are constantly interrupting each other or are constantly changing. In order to ensure that an organization's internal processes are operating as best as possible, they should be identified and balanced against other ordered and established metrics in the other perspectives.

Let's start with my favorite business process, an unintentional process, which has a tendency to run through all the balanced scorecard perspectives. That process is:

"Murphy's Law."

Narrative

Murphy's Law operates within business systems as a hidden process. Its function is to find and leverage hidden flaws that exist within individual processes and, through system effects, interrupt and defeat the process.

*My favorite **Murphy's Law** process story involves printing thousands of plot plans* *for a client. Our task was to generate enlarged plot plans from a master plan and create*

individual autocad drawing files or .dwgs. Late in the delivery, the client decided they

also needed hard copies as well to be developed as well. The task involved sending pre-

generated pdf's to the printer to be printed out as 11x17's. This request, at first

appeared to be a relatively simple task. As outlined, the steps consisted of

1) the drafter would open the dwg, print to a pdf format, and

2) send the pdf to the printer.

However it was soon discovered that one-third to one-half of the thousand of

prints required had discrepancies. Some prints had funny shading on the backgrounds;

others had mashed-up fonts, while others seemed to be missing information that was

correctly shown the dwgs. Our deadline soon loomed and then passed, while we were no

closer to discovering the process error. In response to the missed deadline, we threw

additional staff onto the project, hoping to find the end, but the errors just worsened.

We were at our wits end. Everyone was trying harder and harder to make the plots work,

but the mistakes kept multiplying.

Frustrated, we sat down and delineated the processes steps. Was there anything

wrong with the dwgs? No. A sampling showed that the dwgs (which were developed at a

single offshore facility), were satisfactory. The problem seemed to exist in the pdf

generation and printing.

We asked who was preparing the pdfs? Originally, the offshore team was to

prepare dwgs and then pdfs, which were to be delivered electronically. However when

the scope increased to our onshore team printing hardcopies from the pdfs produced by the facility, we assumed responsibility for packaging the pdf into plottable groups. We also, as part of a last minute modification from the client, became responsible for small modifications for a number of files. We agreed to the modification, since we were plotting the hard copies, it would be easy to open up the dwgs, make the change, make pdfs and plot them. The team also decided to incorporate a pdf packaging program which would make one spoolable file for large quantities of pdfs.

When we reviewed on onshore drafting team's steps for creating a pdf, we found out that each drafter used a slightly different set of steps to create and then print the pdf. We had three drafters. Two used two different types of pdf making freeware; pdf factory, or cutepdf, to create the pdfs. After each pdf was created, it was handed off to the third drafter who used yet another pdf generator which "stapled" the separately created pdfs into a large single file. This program allowed large groups of pdfs to be "packaged" together and spooled to the printer.

The packaging software compressed the separately created files differently depending on whether the file was created by cute pdf or pdf factory, or by the acrobat files created at the facility. The seeming randomness of the errors was actually dutifully created by the third party software, as it collected randomly generated pdfs into a single printable package. Murphy had been introduced into the process system through our adhoc developed steps of creating, packaging and printing pdfs.

Once this was discovered, we were able to quickly process Murphy out of the system. We dedicated one drafter using a dedicated computer and software, the task of sending the multiple facility created pdfs in a queued group (no stapling) to be spooled *to the printer. The pdf's the team had to create separately were created directly with the third party purchased software (not the freeware of cutepdf or pdf factory) and subsequently spooled separately to the printer.*

Murphy disappeared after the first run, and all subsequent hardcopies were correct.

Hidden Murphys

In an adhocractic organization, many processes contain hidden Murphys just waiting for the right pressure or stress to release them. In doing our work, new steps are tried on the fly and organically incorporated into a process. Artful and agile project requirements soon solidify into necessary steps and are applied as common requirements.

Appraising processes includes uncovering and cataloging the steps and tasks that may fail and help develop an understanding of the staff and organizational requirements and an understanding the nature of the process itself.

Future Problem Analysis and the Plan-Do-Check-Act (PDCA) cycle

To help uncover a Murphy, one of the steps of the appraisal should involve uncovering what might go wrong within a process. This review uncovers the effects that individual steps (if they go wrong) may cause to the process and to determine if any of the process steps should be eliminated. Plan-Do-Check-Act is a tool developed by W. Edwards Deming for continuing process improvement. For the architecture firm, I've modified the Deming PDCA cycle to RISMI for — *Review-Identify-Standardize/Stabilize-Measure-Improve*

R I S M I

REVIEW

Review current processes

This step includes identifying the project checklist or checklists and reviewing the project's required deliverables with the team. Ensure that all team members understand the project requirements and what is to be delivered. Then, using the same checklists, the team should review the deliverables (drawings, specifications, cost estimates) for compliance to the checklist items at the end of each phase, or at times the deliverables are submitted. (Note: Although a separate review team provides a new set of eyes; avoid taking away the project team's responsibility for its own checklists and checking. Shigeo Shingo of Toyota instituted a self and successive inspection program where workers inspect their work prior to passing it along to the next worker when it is inspected again. This resulted in reducing assembly-line process errors to near zero.) The review process should detect the differences between compliance and deficiency and make the previous team member aware what is needed for correction (e.g., correction of the deliverables and the processes that led up to the deliverables).

IDENTIFY

Identify process weaknesses or deficiencies

Use results from the review of current processes to determine areas that need improvement such as:

- Information capture and dissemination

- Project requirements

- Consultant coordination

Once the weaknesses have been identified, the firm should take actions necessary to prevent and correct them. Such actions may include further training, additional standardization of work, more explicit instructions, and additional identifiable delivery milestones.

STANDARDIZE/STABILZE

Standardize and stabilize workflow

Pareto theory states that at least 80% of every project consists of standard work involving drawings or processes. Identify that work and processes (partition, door, and opening schedules, abbreviations, ADA mounting heights and clearances, even details such as window and door heads. Standardizing and sharing this information through forms and standardized drawing sheets can free up time and fee in order to spend the remaining 20% of the project requirements, which are unique. Listing process and product standards can mitigate the risk of showing wrong or incomplete information. For example, the project documents can list and draw UL partitions and assemblies, Wood Institute standards for casework, ADA manuals and references for clearances, and contractor and manufacturer trade references for constructability issues. Standardization shouldn't stop at drawings. All business processes should be standard or have significant components, which can be standardized such as:

- Cad files and layering

- Invoicing

- Office Meetings

- Training

Once quality variation has been removed from processes through prevention, the processes should be stabilized. This can be achieved by the use of RCA tools such as VSM. For example, in one variance-prone issue-tracking construction administration process, the team found that a number of issues were being forgotten and unresolved. The VSM process uncovered and corrected handling issues. A spreadsheet and flowchart were developed for team members to track, answer, and route the construction administration issues. Additional improvements were also identified which, in turn, made the system more efficient and stable

MEASURE

Measure performance

Quality cannot be improved without measurement; however, measurement is one of the most overlooked quality steps. Even simple metrics such as registering on-time drawing delivery or error-free client invoices can be an important and successful differentiator for the architectural firm.

Once a system is stabilized, the use of metrics can promote and improve its stability. The firm should establish and track metrics incorporating people, processes, project participants, and finance. Additionally, lagging indicators (e.g., orders filled, training hours spent, and customer retention and referral percentage) should be combined with leading indicators (e.g., orders in process or booked work, and staff enrollment in training) to provide the most accurate measures. Tracking both lagging and leading measures helps ensure that the team and firm have control over their processes and are planning for the future. Auditing is critical to validate everyone's involvement in the program. The audit process identifies problem areas as well as areas of success. An audit program measures and reports against the policy requirements. Examples of QM audits include performance reviews, design audits and reviews, post-occupancy evaluations, and client satisfaction surveys.

IMPROVE

Improving Quality Continuously

As noted earlier, QM is as much about quality improvement as it is about quality maintenance. Once a team or firm has validated that QM policy and program requirements have been met, it strives to further improve the QM functions and processes. Improvements may include such things as faster turnaround times, additional standardized work, and pre-completed drawing sheets. It may also include identifying and revamping processes that aren't adequate for particular clients or projects.

To be successful, quality improvement can't just address processes that management has determined are important. Improvement also calls for creating QM initiatives that build on the ideas of employees. Fostering an innovative firm will help nourish a more effective QM program. Rather than pushing improvement onto project teams, make improvement ideas a feature (if not a requirement) of staff and project meetings. Simple questions, such as "how can we improve this process?" or "what are the operational constraints in finishing this task?" can identify frustrating hurdles that the frontline staff deals with everyday that management may be unaware of.

Keep in mind that small, front-line ideas are the primary means for organizational learning and improvement. Small ideas are also an excellent source for larger ideas, to leverage team, project, and organizational improvement. Creating a QM program, which integrates idea generation as a problem solving and improvement tool acknowledges the ability of frontline staff to leverage small improvements into a creative and evolving organization.

RISMI is key to future-proofing the organization's processes. The **REVIEW and IDENTIFY** steps outline the process's key requirements, the actions, inputs or events that must take place if the implementation is to be successful. Failure of action of any of these requirements will cause problems within the process and system. The review should utilize "negative brainstorming," a cataloging of all things that might and could (or can and will) go wrong. If this cataloging reveals an excess of potential missteps in the process, the review should also include an estimate of risk that each problem may produce.

The **STANDARDIZE/STABILIZE** steps identifies and lists the possible causes for the outlined problems, and the risk results associated with it. This list should include the likelihood that a problem will occur and severity of the impact if it does, so that 'high likelihood / high impact' risks can be anticipated. These activities identify and smooth common-cause variations and try to eliminate special-cause variations through stabilization.

MEASURE creates the metrics for continued monitoring of the process, and **IMPROVE** provides the basis for continual improvements to the processes. For future-proofing the measure and improve steps should identify and develop preventative actions for process problems rather than trying to solve each problem after it happens.

The goals for this analysis are to help teams develop foresight for the impact of future processes and their system effects, as well as to understand the need for contingency plans within existing processes. This analysis identifies adhoc steps which might cause serious negative effects if they're unpreventable, and where other Murphys might be lurking even if the discovered risks are prevented.

Create innovation through the Process perspective

In addition to process appraisal, the process perspective should develop tools to help the firm improve. Within this perspective the architectural firm should seek not only to monitor processes, but to create innovation.

What is innovation? And can processes be modified or developed, that will nourish innovation?

Business Innovation can be simply identified as the act of introducing something new. Within the firm innovative new processes or deliverables are typically created by changes in the balance of market or process forces. Innovation can be introduced by the threat of competition from rival firms, the emergence of new and unrealized market opportunities, changes in business philosophy, changes in management structure, new capabilities within the firm, or even changes within the economy.

The process of introducing an innovation begins by creating a methodology which supports innovation, as in developing a process which tries to solve a problem or realize a new opportunity. The famous economist, Joseph Schumpeter outlined a theory of "creative destruction" which delineates the difference between

1) invention,

2) innovation, and

3) imitation.

His theory is built on the fact that it is difficult to change the routines of an established and sustaining process or economic system. He stated that "The opening up of new markets and the organizational development illustrate the process of industrial mutation that incessantly revolutionizes the economic structure from within, incessantly destroying the old one, incessantly creating a new one ... [The process] must be seen in its role in the perennial gale of creative destruction; it cannot be understood on the hypothesis that there is a perennial lull."

Which is why, now in 2009, the automobile companies are embracing and promoting alternative fuel (even pure electric) vehicles, where five years earlier they were famously crushing electric cars. Therefore, successful innovation must compete with existing systems and processes until it is embraced as the way things are. Which may be too late for some legacy players (see Tower Records, and Montgomery Ward, then; GM and Chrysler, now).

The activities which eventually rupture these systems is described as a disruptor. The global economic meltdown that began in 2007 became the disruptor for all incumbent technologies, business models and processes. Other disruptors occur within the industry and incorporate the technology it will eventually eliminate. Familiar examples of disruptors include cellphones to landlines, email to faxes, and ipods to cds. In each of these cases an innovation initially built on the incumbent technology, and then eventually replaced it.

Create Innovation

In creating a scorecard that supports **innovation,** the firm creates basic startup metrics which identify and support disruptors:

1)   **type and degree** of innovation

2)   **product innovation** – what is offered

3)   **process innovation** – how it is created or delivered

4)   **service innovation** – how is the delivery different from existing service deliveries

5)   **degree of "novelty"** – is the innovation incremental, radical and disruptive

6)   **primary source of innovation** – 'technology-push' v. 'market pull'

A process scorecard which focuses on leveraging a disruptive technology should engage the customer perspective by recognizing that a new process is initially presented to the firm's lead customer as an extension to the existing service offering. An organization typically responds to this reaction by continuing to achieve customer validation of its existing processes and offering subsequently deferring complete implementation of the disruptive technology. It will instead marginally update or add components in order to achieve the endorsement of the existing technology.

Why is active management of innovation ideas so important? Why? -

-85% of new ideas never reach a market

-60% of R&D projects are market failures

-40% of consumer products and services fail

-40% of alliances fail to deliver objectives

-30% of technology-based new ventures fail

-20% of business products and services fail

If a firm wants to create and support a new technology, it initially should be a part of an existing technology.

Innovation rating

Level 1 Innovation: Surface Innovation (no invention). This level of innovation implements already established solutions in order to solve an existing problem. An example of a Level 1 implementation is making exterior walls thicker in order to achieve greater insulation thickness.

Level 2: Improvement Innovation. This innovation is the adding small improvements to an existing system, but still maintaining existing compromises within the existing system. An example of a Level 2 improvement would be the addition of a stopwatch function to a digital watch.

Level 3: Invention inside an existing system. This is an innovation characterized as the implementation of essential improvements to an existing system. An example of a Level 3 improvement is changing a manual transmission to an automatic transmission.

Level 4: Invention outside the system. This is an innovation of a new generation of processes which changes the primary function processes. An example of a Level 4 improvement is the new use of nutrient blockers in cancer tumor therapy. The idea of starving a tumor to death by cutting off its blood and nutrient supply is a Level 4 improvement.

Level 5: Discovery Innovation. This is a pioneer invention of a new system which is completely outside the existing system. Transistors and semiconductors are examples of a Level 5 improvement.

Level 6: Adaption Innovation. This is the successful imitation of an innovation outside of the system's industry which is newly adapted to a new industry. Examples include Lean processes. With a level 6 Adaption innovation, since there is no separate distinction between innovation and imitation/diffusion, the innovative contents of adaption become the disruptor.

Schumpeterian Creative Destruction

Schumpeterian theory state that customers and market demand alone cannot create successful innovation. A firm must actively create support and value chains for the innovation. They must also help facilitate processes to foster innovation, rather than wait for client requests. Most clients may not see the point of supporting a firm's interest in trying to use a disruptor, as they are just interested in successful transactions.

Existing technology and the client's routine behavior frame the demand side of the market. Therefore the firm must act as a champion for the innovation in order to drive change and persuade its clients to modify their behavior and preferences. The **success of a disrupter depends on the value chains** created by these champions and their lead users, its niche and early adopters, who require advanced or modified performance and be convinced to help support the disruptor rather than the status quo.

Niche and Early Adopter Success

After realizing niche and early adopter success the disruptor begins to move up-market and pushes the innovation into the realm of the established technology.

Thus, the disruptive lifecycle, can be outlined as follows:

1)   Invention of a disruptor in an incumbent organization

2)   Presentation of the disruptor to the incumbent customers

3)   Initial rejection of the disruptor by the incumbent's lead customers

4)   The sustaining organization adding features to the incumbent technology in order to sustain market share

5)   Niche or narrowly focused marketing of disrupter by firms outside the incumbent establishment.

6)   Market success of disruptor

7)   Belated acceptance and marketing of disruptor by the incumbent organization

Because an innovation's final application is unknown at its inception, its successful deployment must be nourished and monitored through a process scorecard. A scorecard advancing innovation identifies and develops metrics for the application of new techniques for old tools and the generation of new processes. It also establishes allowance for failure which formalizes that the disruptor and supporting team receives leveraged opportunities over a certain period of time in order to identify markets and achieve success for the disruptor.

In creating and supporting the disruptor, the firm should

1) anticipate the disruptor's needs and requirements and respond and adapt

2) capture ideas from outside the firm

3) learn from past projects

4) identify performance measurement and key indicators

5) develop value-added services to support the innovation

6) build and maintain the firm's reputation

7) integrate business and project processes

8) find a match between current ways of working, formal procedures and creative forward thinking approaches

Initiative	Perspective	Objective	Lag Measure	Lead Measure	Target
Innovation	Financial	Build diverse teams into fee breakdowns.			
	Customers	Introduce Diverse Team to Clients			
	Processes	Integrate new staff through existing studios			
	People	Hire cognitively diverse staff			

Balanced Spreadsheet for Innovation

0.5 People	Training	List items here that promote training	100%	85%	0.425
1 Processes	Internal	List items here that promote improvement of processes	100%	95%	0.95
1.5 Customer	Client touch	New client initiatives	100%	95%	1.425
2 Financial	New business	Pricing or colletions	100%	95%	1.9
6				5.70	95%

The following table describes the current payout:

Score		Payout	Annualized
0 - 49.9%		$ -	$ -
50 - 59.9%		$ -	$ -
60 - 69.9%		$ -	$ -
70 - 84.9%		$ 100.00	#######
85 - 94.9%		$ 300.00	#######
> 95%		$ 500.00	#######

Narrative. It seems like my firm, a large multi-office national player, will focus on one thing per month; this month it's sustainability and another thing next month. As a young project-architect, I feel like we're bouncing from idea to idea with no connection to anything previous or planned. It would be nice if somehow all this stuff was somehow linked, and finance knew it was funded, marketing knew we were promoting it, and HR knew how to hire for it. It would also be nice if our Project Managers were provided with tools to make it work, and we were all given training that supported us learning it.

Changing the quality focus paradigm within a firm

If a firm wants to be innovative and change its process offerings in the marketplace, where does it start? How does it catalog and leverage the expertise of its staff into a business development skill?

In this example, we look at a firm trying to position itself as a quality management leader in the industry – how should it go about understanding what it does with what it knows and then mitigate what it doesn't while leveraging what it does. Quality-control within a design firm is typically accomplished through a brute force document inspection activity performed at the end of identified production phases.

Quality science demonstrates that a firm cannot *inspect-in* quality. Either a firm generates and delivers quality documents through its successful internal processes, or it tries to catch process errors through inspection. However, an inspection-only process can only find and locate a small sampling of errors in an average set of construction documents. Adding levels of inspections (through new-sets of eyes, or checking the checkers), actually creates additional errors. **Multiple inspections become less reliable as each subsequent inspector depends on the next inspector to catch missed errors.** Divided inspection therefore divides responsibility.

With that in mind, how should a firm review its existing processes within a quality management framework? Most of a firm's processes develop organically over the years in response to customer project and financial requirements. In a quality-based organization, can legacy processes that have developed over time capture and leverage everything the firm now knows?

Powerful Statement of Intent

In reviewing its QM focus, it is important that the entire organization understands and affirms the review and mission for change.

Therefore the review should begin with a powerful statement of intent:

Inspection-only QA/QC cannot be tolerated as part of this organization's strategic vision.

If the organization tries to implement change without this vision statement firmly mandated and endorsed, then that the planned change will turn into just another flavor of the month.

What are the next steps?

Rather than embrace the vision, some leaders of the firm may feel that inspection is adequate but just needs to be performed by different individuals. Other leaders may feel that there is too much inspection and that it occurs during the wrong phases of the project. Still others may believe that there is nothing wrong with the inspection process, and that there are no problems with QA/QC, but that the problems lie with an inexperienced and unsupervised staff.

In order to create the most successful plan available, the design firm must first identify the problems within the existing QA/QC processes. Only then can the firm begin to consider solutions.

Continual past failures in QA/QC activities have demonstrated a lack of focus, commitment and understanding as to what QA/QC is and what it should accomplish. Understanding and agreeing what the problems are is paramount prior to developing a mandate for change.

One way to develop an organizational understanding and to create a mandate is tease out the hidden beliefs and competencies within the firm. Cataloging the knowledge (institutional intrinsic, and personal extrinsic) and then building training programs understanding how training can be best led, can be accomplished by utilizing *concept mapping*. Developed in the 1960s by Joseph D. Novak at Cornell, concept mapping is a tool that graphically represents the structural or core knowledge of the firm. This intrinsic institutional knowledge provides the conceptual basis for explaining why things are they way they are within an organization. Concept mapping graphically uncovers how the organization's existing prior knowledge and belief systems are interconnected and combined. It is a tool to help identify the framework of the organization's culture.

Different from brainstorming, concept mapping helps uncover the firm's intrinsic core knowledge in order to generate new ideas, communicate complex themes, and aid group learning by explicitly and publically integrating existing and new group knowledge. It allows a firm to assess understanding within the staff and to diagnose misunderstanding within systems and processes.

While there are numerous tools for implementing concept mapping, for our review we will utilize Card Sorting.

Card Sorting.

Card sorting is a four-step group activity that facilitates the collection of organizational knowledge through a neutral forum. Card sorting reduces the possibility of management bias by assisting a diverse group of the firm's staff and management designate what is critical to the organization and what is not.

First Step.

The first step in card sorting is to gather a group together to generate problem statements (card sorting can also be used with Appreciative Inquiry, in which case the team would utilize its Ai statements). The group should consist of at least twelve and not more than twenty people from all departments and disciplines within the firm. In the architecture firm, this should include the Drafters, the Project Architects and Managers, the Administration Staff, Accounting, Printing Staff, Construction Administration Staff, and the Executive Leadership. A complete and diverse group will ensure that important issues and themes won't be overlooked. The card-sorting group, with a team facilitator, identifies issues around the problem statements. For example, if the group was examining quality control issues, the problem statements would read: not enough spec writers, or not enough time to finish the construction drawings, or, would like more-contractor input into the details. Through discussion, the group will identify problems and issues, and describe each one as briefly as possible on separate 3"x5" card.

Second Step

The second step is to complete a group edit of the Problem Statements. The reviewing group should review each statement for clarity and duplication. The group should also edit each Problem Statement as necessary. If more than 50 problems are identified, the group should divide the problems into separate groups of 50 or so, by general content areas. As part of this step, the reviewing group should then copy each Problem

Statement onto multiple 3x 5 index cards. The group should copy enough cards so that

each member of the group will have a complete set of statement cards. Add 5 to 10

blank cards to each deck so additional problem statements can be added as the group

completes the meeting.

Third Step

The third step is the Card-Sorting session. The group should meet at tables outfitted

with plenty of blank newsprint sheets and markers. There should be at least three

tables. The Card-Sorting session has five steps.

Present Background Information. The group facilitator should present a 10 to 15 minute

summary of background information relating to the major issues of concern regarding

QA/QC (the war stories) to the group. All members of the group should be listening to

the presentation.

Review Problem Statements. Have each person review his set of cards. The facilitator

instructs the group members to add any additional problems, concerns, or issues that

that they believe are important which are not included in the deck. Everyone in the

group should add these new problem statements on the blank cards provided. Each

member's deck should be identical.

Sort Cards. Each person then sorts their cards into three piles - - "yes," "no," and "maybe" - - depending on how important they feel each problem is to the organization. Everyone then goes through their "yes" pile and selects the 5 statements that they consider to be most important. It is not necessary to rank these five choices.

Rank Problems by Tables. Each group member in turn names one of their top five problems. These are recorded on the newsprint at the table. The procedure is repeated until everyone's top five have been recorded on newsprint. The people around the table vote to select the top five of the table. The top five are listed on newsprint.

Total Group Discussion. The facilitator then collects the top 5 problem statements from each table and makes a master list on newsprint - - not in any special order. The problems are numbered consecutively, and each discussed in turn. - why did each of the tables think the problems listed are important?

Fourth Step.
The fourth step is a group vote on the problem statements. The meeting should end with the entire group voting, either by a show of hands or by taking an "exit poll." Each person in attendance should identify or list the 5 problems she/he thinks are most important - - again, not in any special order. After the meeting, the facilitator tabulates the results and informs the participants what problem statement and priorities were established as a result of the meeting.

Conclusion

Facilitated correctly, Card Sorting will confirm or refute firm knowledge concerning the issue begin reviewed by the firm. It will clarify and prioritize the issues in order and create an action plan for directioned change. The resulting date can be ordered into cluster diagrams, hierarchical maps, or affinity diagrams. Card Sorting prepares the organization in planning for a change initiative.

Lean enterprise tools and the practice of architecture

Lean enterprise tools and the practice of architecture

Narrative. It would be great if my firm could take techniques that have been used in factories or manufacturing and modify them for use in our office. I don't know how, and I know it wouldn't match the creative side of what we do, but…I mean, I know we're like, creative and unable to tie down, but it would be really interesting to see how we could take something like the assembly line and implement parts into our production techniques.

KANBANS for agency review

Drawing Kanbans for OSHPD

Kanbans have been used in Lean Manufacturing and Production since first introduced by Toyota as part of its Just-In-Time manufacturing process. The Toyota Production System (TPS) is world famous for its ability to produce high quality products on demand. *Kanban* is a Japanese term for "signal." It is used in Lean Manufacturing as a way to track **work-in-process** production. It signals a cycle of production and materials and is used to maintain an orderly and efficient flow of materials throughout a production process. In manufacturing, it usually takes the shape of a printed card that contains specific information such as part name, description and quantity.

How to use the Kanban system for drawing production

For almost 30 years, architects have utilized 2d CAD systems which don't easily allow for active traditional "over-the-shoulder" in-progress oversight review. With CAD, drawing review can only be measured by stopping production, and then printing and reviewing, and then starting over again. Because of the interface requirements of 2d CAD, with its multiple overlay and xrefing requirements, it is almost impossible to determine without hardcopy. An inventory kanban system can be used to review CAD drawing progress. The following case example illustrates how effective a kanban system can be.

OSHPD

The California Office of Statewide Health Planning and Development (OSHPD) provides review and inspection of hospital construction. Once the construction documents have been approved and permitted by OSHPD, any change must be tracked and collected into Post-Approval Documents (PAD). These documents are submitted to OSHPD by the architect in order to outline the revisions.

In addition to showing revised drawings, the PAD review process requires the submittal of a narrative document which describes the revisions and explains the reasons for the changes. The narrative is a required deliverable made for the benefit of the OSHPD reviewer who formally reviews and approves the changes, be they Request for Information (RFI) responses or owner changes. This document is submitted along with the revised drawings. The drawings themselves must have each revision properly clouded and identified (with numbered deltas).

OSHPD is stringent concerning these requirements, if a PAD is submitted that has changes without benefit of narrative or proper description and version control, the submittal is summarily rejected.

How the Kanban was implemented.

Our project carried a $1 billion price tag for 1.2 million square-feet of a new full-service hospital space. The OSHPD permit package consisted of more than 3,000 sheets of drawings, and over 1,500 pages of specifications, schedules and other small-sized documents. For our project the **OSHPD Post Approval Document (PAD)** change consisted of owner revisions, contractor changes or architectural instructions which

incorporates anywhere from 30 to 200 sheets of changed documents. Additionally, our

project engaged four separate design firms, plus mechanical, electrical, plumbing, and

structural engineering services as well as other consultants actively involved in

producing revisions.

Our team's first effort at creating a PAD submittal resulted in 100% failure. We

submitted a revised drawing package which contained revisions that weren't clouded or

described in the narrative, drawings which had mixed revision clouds or reference

numbers (past, present and future), as well as narrations which didn't match the

revisions (and vice-versa). All drawings and disciplines were affected. It turned out, that

during the revision process, these changes were too scattered to be trackable and

traceable. Our team wasn't able to string the pieces of the revisions together coherently

enough to package the PAD; our team couldn't describe the changes, and couldn't

manage a process which turned out to be too disparate and transient to successfully

collect and catalog.

Subsequently OSHPD immediately rejected the submittal.

In reviewing the failure and proposing a fix, the team faced with the ***inspecting-in quality*** solution dilemma.

A delivery failure in architecture is listed as a quality control failure and therefore an inspection error. Each failure follows the same course: An inexperienced team, with limited supervision, delivers a drawing package which turns out to be incomplete and uncoordinated. Lack of inspection, prior to delivery, is identified as the problem and an oversight group is quickly convened and engaged to *"fix the problem"* In response to the failure, a monitoring group is created, usually separate from the project team, and third-party inspection schedules are generated and identified against an identified delivery checklist for all future deliveries.

Unfortunately, this is a classic failure response model for the architectural firm, complete with blame, villains, heroes and deadline goals, repeated earnestly in all firms. This is a reactive program, initially mitigating the important surface quality problems; the low-hanging fruit of quality management. This is the missing information and the lack of coordination between disciplines. But this type of inspection only fixes errors after they have been made.

In manufacturing quality programs, this *fixing-after-the-fact* is called Rework. Rework does nothing to fix drawing problems during production of the drawings. Additionally this type of inspection and rework isn't sustainable because the time and expense of additional inspectors, and drawing things twice or three times can't be built into the process. There must be an inspection process, but each team member must be empowered to self-inspect prior to handing the process over. In our kanban example, the final inspection is OSHPD, with no rework allowed.

Kanbans

In this project, the team outlined the idea of a production *Kanban.* This kanban wouldn't check the completion or coordination of the process, it wouldn't magically bring outside inspectors into the team, but it would help the team manage and self-inspect their process.

The team created a Word document template that matched the approved OSHPD narrative form (see figures). Instructions were given to all members of the team that when they opened a live drawing and began making changes they were to attach (embed) the Word document into the CAD sheet and begin filling it in as they completed the changes. Columns in the template identified each revision, and outlined the reason for the change and stated the number the revision would receive for that CAD sheet.

When the team member was finished with changes for that document or complete for the day, they would complete the form and save the document along with the drawings. The drafter would also select and copy the information into an email and mail the changes to a designated PAD e-mailbox. The subject line of each email was designated so that each email would sort itself into each sheet or specification or schedule change, who made the change, and the date the change was made. The kanban even specified what format the email should use; only rich-text email file types were allowed.

When the team prepared a PAD change-package they would go to the email folder and select the emails describing the appropriate document changes. For example, if several different team members worked on drawing A.302, the selection process would pick all emails with A.302 as the subject reference line. The PAD packager would open up all the emails for the selected PAD and copy the text from each one. If the emails were formatted incorrectly or of the wrong file type, the packager would reject the email and send it back to the team member for correction prior to packaging.

To work properly, the ***Kanban* should be simple**. This change-handling process demonstrated that the any member of the project team, as well as management, could determine what revisions had been made with a quick review of email files. The email *Kanban* could be used to describe the changes to the engineering team, and the CAD sheet with attached *Kanban* could be sent to each discipline with the new embedded background.

Occasionally, numerous project members may have participated in a particular change but not fully comprehended the full scope of changes now required as part of the revision, causing co-ordination errors. The changing of a door location, for instance, may have created phase one modifications (interior finishes, electrical switches, thermostat locations, door/hardware changes, etc.), as well as unforeseen phase 2 structural or MEP modifications.

The relationship of the phase 1 changes may not be completely thought through or coordinated throughout the project and subsequent disciplines (and in our case, the other architect's requirements). The kanban reminded the team of the revisions.

For PAD packaging, the selected emails would be collected from the email folder and opened. Each email would be copied and pasted into a master PAD narrative. Because the email formatting was consistent, the final document required minimal editing and could be printed to use as a checklist for reviewing the PAD documents. Once the drawings were published, the changes were frozen and the word document detached. The drawings were placed back into the server for active revisions. When new revisions were required, the team member would attach a fresh Word template and begin the process anew.

Once these protocols were implemented, including attaching active and traceable changes to the drawings, a self-audit trail was formed, Packaging and inspection was reduced initially by 50% (1 to 2 team members) and once the firm achieved complete compliance with the new protocols, the reduction increased to 70-80% (4 team members.)

The use of Kanbans in non-PAD document production.

After realizing success in its limited utilization with PAD revisions, the team was asked if it could think of ways to implement the system into the typical production of construction documents. Since PAD documents were discrete and traceable overlays to existing documents, developing and using *Kanbans* was easy. Would using *Kanbans* to signal typical progress of a drawing set be seen as too difficult and oppressive? Since narratives aren't a traditional requirement of drawing production, asking a team member to write down and email everything they had done for the day could prove to be a difficult task if not required and enforced from the production side. Creating a daily narrative would be a way to track time, project completion, and coordination efforts. It would also be a way to create standardized work, matching the RISMI cycle.

This OSHPD project demonstrated that *Kanbans* could be incorporated into the control of production and inventory of drawings and other construction documents. The success realized by moving quality control from an inspection process to a work in-progress production process was especially important as it outlined new methods firms could try to integrate quality processes into project development and production.

Initiative	Perspective	Objective	Lag Measure	Lead Measure	Target
Innovation	Financial	Build diverse teams into fee breakdowns.			
	Customers	Introduce Diverse Team to Clients			
	Processes	Integrate new staff through existing studios			
	People	Hire cognitively diverse staff			

LEAN PROCESSES FOR ARCHITECTURAL SERVICES

Lean Value Stream Mapping of Construction Administration Processes

This chapter outlines how to implement Lean Enterprise tools to review and fix process issues. Our case study utilizes a review of field trailer submittal and RFI review processes for the construction administration design team. The existing system was a classic legacy batch and queue process, which relied on the collection and distribution of submittals and RFI's, creating an inventory process problem.

We first began by tackling the process of submittal review, which included contractor provided shop, fabrication and installation drawings, product data cut sheets, and product samples.

Knowledge of Variation

We started at the beginning, following the Lean production outline established in James Womack and Daniel Jones' book: <u>Lean Thinking</u>, which listed the review steps as - 1)identify value, 2)map the value stream, and 3)establish flow. Once the flow is established, the team should institute 4)customer pull, and then pursue 5)perfection.

W. Edwards Deming taught the fundamentals that became Lean to the Japanese after WWII. He outlined a theory which included "Knowledge of Variation." Tools within this theory required an organization to confirm the type of variation within a firm's organization processes. Deming stated that there were two types of variation:

1) Common-cause (or normal) variation, and

2) Special Variation.

Common-cause variations within our project included the project type and setup requirements, including planned project delivery and construction methods. A process balanced scorecard should facilitate the architectural firm in identifying and planning for all common-cause variables. These variations should be measurable and part of the system, controllable by management and identifiable and definable to staff.

Special cause variations are the unexpected deviations which occur outside the planned system's processes. For the architectural firm special cause variations include new or inexperienced team members, new and unfamiliar project types, new construction processes or delivery requirements. Additional sources of special cause variations might include a change to the project by an outside force such an unexpected agency or owner change. The firm should understand that a special cause variation is an outside variable that is unexpected to the existing processes and systems of the project; it is not the same as nor can it be treated like a normal process variation. Identifying, controlling and minimizing both types of variation are important parts of the process perspective.

Work Application/Process

Fix the Site Trailer – Lean Process

Narrative. Sometimes, in my firm, it feels like we do the same wrong thing over and over again. It means that we have systems in place that are built around processes that existed years ago and are no longer useful. One really good example of this is the processing of contractor RFIs (requests for information) and shop drawing submittals.

Five years ago everything was hard copies, with binders and notebooks and piles of folded-up yellowing drawings. The organization for these documents seemed like it was something that was set up generations ago by a harried file clerk in the dungeons of some long-lost government office.

Now the file cabinets, the stamp pads, the endless rolls of drawings with splitting rubber bands—it seems all so retro.

Now, we're in the early 21st century, we've moved beyond sepia and blue-lined hard copies, but all of our dusty 19th century filing systems are still in place. We, as an industry, have overlaid a digital veneer over the ammonia and light tables of the past. The delivery system seems almost steam-punk...

Shouldn't we just start over?

Value Stream Mapping

Value Stream Mapping

Value Stream Mapping is a technique that was first utilized by Toyota to help its workers identify and review value streams rather than discrete processes and operations.

Implementing mapping is a process where the first step involves outlining the current flow of materials or information in the business's key processes. The mapping is done with the help of flowcharts that depict the flow of goods or information from beginning to end. The flowchart also contains information about the average time taken for the completion of various sub processes. For generating a comprehensive value stream flowchart participants gather inputs from the business heads, managers and administrative staff.

While creating the map, **key sub-processes are highlighted using specific icons**. This helps in pinpointing areas where waste and inconsistencies are happening. The flowchart also helps in understanding the complexity of the business process, which needs to be simplified for increasing efficiency.

Future State Value Stream Mapping

In the next phase, mapping participants review each step depicted in the flowchart in order to find ways to streamline and optimize the process. A number of methods can be used during the future state mapping process but only those that help in streamlining processes without affecting the day-to-day operations of an organization should be selected.

Takt Time is one method that is used for evaluating lead-time of deliverables or services. Takt Time measures the time of flow through the process. A Takt Time map is useful if the team is measuring the flow of time sensitive information through the system (like RFIs or Shop drawings). In a takt time process, Kanbans can be used to perform VSM as a way to help maintain low inventory levels. We utilized a kanban map in our OSHPD system

Mini Golf
Submittal and RFI (Request for Information) Flow and Tracking or why a project is like a game of mini-golf.

We conducted a value stream mapping session on submittal and RFI flow and tracking: A value stream map consists of identifying all the steps that make the process work.

In order to begin the process, the firm must identify the current state map. Our current state map began with statement that our trailer team lost track of where submittals and RFIs were in the review queue.

Our current state value map found a number of system problems. These included fundamental tracking control issues including identification of which team had reviewed, which team had returned, where are the documents filed, and if a re-submittal is required, and where to find the first copy for back-check comparison.

Additionally we found that the system handled a minimum of several hundred RFIs and at least fifty submittals a week. The project's logging system was an online system which only the contractor actively utilized. Each design review team utilized their own logging and tracking system. In each case it was a rudimentary spreadsheet, which relied on the construction architect to export all required information from the system into a trackable

The current state map outlined a number of issues including - System Requirements. Internal and External verification of Reviewing Logs, Organizing hardcopy filing for retrieval, establishing tracking, and providing meaningful follow-up and feedback for the design team and the Contractor and Construction Manager

Submittals:

All submittals (shop drawings) followed the legacy hardcopy process established back with sepias and blueprints. This is based on the past requirements of "6 copies and a sepia (which we short-handed as 6CS). This means that although this particular project (3,000 individual and separate sheets of 36" x 48" drawings) is 100% produced through Computer Aided Drafting (CAD) software, the specified and contracted submittal requirement is for hardcopy.

The delivery of Submittals is a requirement of the contract specifications to assure that the contractor is supplying the specified information. That requirement too, is based on the hand drawn method of thirty years ago. Thus, the contractor delivers 6CS so that the reviewing team member can review and mark up all copies (including the reproducible sepia) and deliver the package back to the Contractor (through the Construction Manager), who in turn distributes the package to his/her workforce for installation, revision, and/or re-submittal.

Value Map: The Contractor introduces the 6CS, into the system as follows:

1)   Contract is Awarded.

2)   Contractor notifies subcontractor of specification requirement of 6CS.

3)   Contractor receives 6CS package from subcontractor and logs into Prolog.

4)   Contractor transmits 6CS to Construction Manager (CM)

5)   CM logs 6CS into Expedition, and bundles 6CS into package for delivery to design team (through the architect).

6)   Architect receives 6CS and logs entry into Prolog and delivers package to design team members for review.

7)   Design Team review members throw away 6 C's (Six copies), and begins reviews (first value added component) and marks up sepia.

8)   Design Team makes copy of sepia for file and sends sepia back to Architect.

9)   Architect receives package, logs package into Prolog, makes copy of sepia for file, and transmits sepia package to CM.

10)   CM receives, logs into Expedition makes 6 copies of marked up sepia and transmits the remains of the 6CS package back to Contractor.

11)   Contractor logs package into Prolog and delivers 6CS to Subcontractor.

12)   Process starts over again.

The purpose of a VSM is to identify the value-added and non-value added processes in the system. The non-value added processes are referred to as muda in a VSM (muda is the Japanese word for waste). From the review of the current-state VSM, muda is found in the bulk of the process in making copies and waiting. In outlining a future state, perfection map, the contractor wouldn't even submit drawings for the design team to review, he would install the work in accordance with the contract documents and require no designer review except for approved installation.

In most projects, the contractor is required by the contract to submit shop drawings in order to demonstrate his understanding of the project. So, if the architect's construction documents are clear enough, the submittal and review process would occur with little or minimal handling time. Near perfection in the Womack and Jones value stream would mean that a submittal should be transmitted directly to the design team who should be able to quickly review it, endorse and deliver it back to the contractor for installation. The processing time (or takt time), between contractor, designer, and back again, should be minimal and effortless.

We found that in our current stream map, we had to redefine the value of the process. Remember the Womack and Jones steps -1)identify value, 2)map the value stream, and 3)establish flow, 4)create customer pull, and then pursue 5)perfection. In order for us to redefine our current stream map we had to identify the value of the process.

Therefore the team stated that the **"value of the submittal review process is to allow the contractor to demonstrate his understanding of the project requirements."** That was it, it wasn't an opportunity for the architect to make last minute changes, and it wasn't a chance for the contractor to introduce a substitution. Mapping the value stream from that perspective allowed us to first eliminate a large quantity of submittal requirements (ceiling grid samples, for example), and focus more on using the submittal process as a communication tool. For example, in order to confirm understanding of the curtain-wall system, shop drawings as well as full scale mockups and additional sealant information may be required. Mapping the stream allowed the team to focus on the important details of the building, rather than receiving the piles of unnecessary samples and boiler-plate drawings. Once the value was established, the team looked to establish flow. How should we receive the drawings? Are hard copies still required? How should we maintain our record copies?

The next step, **create customer pull**, involved identifying who the customer was. With submittals, all parties involved in the creation and review were considered customers. The first customer was the contractor receiving the drawings and buying out the project. The design team became the next customer, as the contractor developed drawings (or samples) to be delivered for review. Customers to the design team may include the owner, the reviewing agency, and the end users of the building. In the end of the cycle, the contractor again becomes the customer, receiving the reviewed submittal back again to be incorporated into the project.

The takt time cycle is developed at the pace of the reviewing team and the project's construction speed. The contract places submittals at a 2 week turn-around cycle. So a submittal coming into queue would be logged in and follow the speed of the reviewer. Eliminating the unnecessary submittals standardized the takt time. We also found it helpful to use real-world processes to help understand how lean works.

Like a game of miniature golf.

There are a number of tools out in the world that help teams understand how lean processes are different than traditional processes. The Lean Construction Institute (LCI) uses the airplane game. The goal is to show that utilizing queuing theory, there is a flow and rhythm to production and services. I like to use mini-golf as my example. Everyone has played mini-golf with a pack of people. Usually it's a birthday party or a summer diversion. Traditional mini-golf is played like real golf. Each person takes a turn in order for every hole. Jack starts off, takes a shot, Mike follows, Beth follows, and so on until the whole group has taken their first shot. Then Jack takes shot two, then Mike, then Beth, etc. **Each hole is finished at the speed of the slowest golfer**.

That's why mini-golf is such a diversion; it's a classic time-suck. Nine holes with eight people can take three hours (I have four children, and have been to way too many mini-golf birthday parties). However if you were to play the game supporting the fastest player, and everyone else queuing up behind and following individually, you can finish nine holes of mini-golf with eight people in twenty minutes. But what's the point of that? The value of mini-golf is to socialize, tease, talk, make trick shots, and so on. The value of mini-golf is not to finish the game as quickly as possible. If it were, everyone would be following on like a rocket, with a nice easy no catch-up rhythm. The problem is that we typically schedule our projects as if they were a mini-golf game.

Barriers to lean: In our case-study, there were several obvious barriers to the near perfection process,

1) The Construction Manager (required as a conduit for submittals),

2) The two different proprietary enterprise systems (Prolog and Expedition, both systems which don't easily communicate with each other.

3) The hard copy push. If submittals are going to flow, then the team must fix the 6CS mindset first.

What Barriers were we able to change based on contracts, agreements, and requirements?

We couldn't change:

1) The CM review and,

2) The enterprise software.

3) The review requirements.

What we changed.
What we were able to change?

1) The Hard Copy Push,

2) The 6CS format.

3) The file and retrieval system

This initial investigation led to review the existing flow (See attachments), which formally confirmed our observations of **muda.** A meeting was convened with the process team where they were asked what ideas they could offer for "outlining and improving the current situation (See attachments). However, their ideas were offered to try to fix their portion of the system (document flow and tracking) and kept the 6CS model intact. After highlighting the "value added portions of the value stream", the staff agreed that the proposed modification was a system work-around, and not a system that introduced a new paradigm.

A review of the contract documents confirmed the requirements of an electronic deliverable from the contractor, so the team's first obligation was to remind the contractor of his/her demand to follow the electronic requirement. As part of this review, the second obligation was for the design and CM team to agree to waive the requirements for hard copy (6CS) review.

Was this feasible? The design team experience with RFIs led the way.

Requests for Information

Request for Information (RFI) is a construction communication tool which the contractor utilizes to obtain contract document interpretation from the design team. In accordance with the specification the contractor asks question utilizes a letter sized form that follows the same flow as described in the submittal process above.

1)   Subcontractor forwards to contractor

2)   Contractor reviews forwards to CM

3)   CM reviews, forwards to Architect

4)   Architect Reviews, forwards to Design Team member

5)   Design team member answers, returns response to Architect.

6)   Architect reviews, logs in, returns response to CM.

7)   CM reviews, logs in, returns to Contractor

8)   Contractor receives, reviews, logs in, and returns to Subcontractor.

RFIs began their life in the same pre-cad world as drawings. However, their compact (8.5" x 11") format has allowed them to migrate from **hard copy push, to electronic pull**. Faxing RFIs in 1990s began this process. Fax scanning software (where faxes are delivered electronic) continued this process, and now scanning software and pdf's in addition to robust project management webtools, allow an RFI to begin and end its life electronically with every reviewer participating in the receipt, review, filing, printing and rescanning of the information. Now an RFI question/response can be attached to an email message and attached to an enterprise project software entry.

Thus RFI communication on this project became electronic almost effortlessly. In fact, detailed RFIs requiring sketches and multiple reviews were able to be produced in such formats that allow the RFI to keep its compact integrity.

However, we realized that before we tried to introduce a new process to the system, we had to fix the old system, similar to the advice **Taiichi Ohno gave in his book, Toyota Production System, "Too much information throws the production field into confusion."**

Summary: Was the "Leaning" of the "Submittal/RFI process at the trailer a success?

Did it work?

Value (The only value added is the review)

Value mapping (Identified and eliminated the significant muda in the system)

Introduce pull. The contractor sends the submittal/RFI so pull is already established.

Push is looked to be reduced by reviewing the submittal electronically.

Establish Flow (the bin time has been reduced)

Pursue perfection (still pursuing)

Initiative	Perspective	Objective	Lag Measure	Lead Measure	Target
Innovation	Financial	Build diverse teams into fee breakdowns.			
	Customers	Introduce Diverse Team to Clients			
	Processes	Integrate new staff through existing studios			
	People	Hire cognitively diverse staff			

Utilizing Organizational Networks to leverage Business Development (and Innovation)

Leveraging organizational creativity: innovative behavior within a design firm.

Narrative

I sometimes surf before work. As I'm finishing up at 9am and changing into my work clothes, I see every sort of individual in the parking lot. Every sort of individual is there: lawyers, accountants, fast food clerks, hair dressers, and students. What established this concept was a conversation I had with this one guy. He was a true dawn-patroller, always out in the surf at first light every morning, and packing it in before nine am. He said he was a flooring contractor, and that he had met all of his past, present, and hopefully, future clients while surfing. His current girlfriend, a flight attendant for a national airline, he had also met after surfing, right here in this parking. He had just come back from two week of surfing to Costa Rica where he had bummed a flight with her.

Surfing was not just his life, but also his business development program. By creating, utilizing, and leveraging his ever-changing soft and weak contacts, his marketing plan was to just continue doing what he liked to do, and build relationships (and business) along the way.

ONIT?

Continuously innovating existing and new business processes is required for firm growth. As a firm's ability to compete on price alone is reduced, the capability to adopt and diffuse an innovative business process becomes critical.

In this chapter we review how a firm can understand and implement the concepts and tools of **Social Network Analysis and Organizational Network Innovation Diffusion Theory (ONIT)** in order to identify, map and leverage a business process innovation within their firm?

What is Social Network Analysis? It is the study of loose social and organizational ties that link ideas and concepts together through knowledge communities. Initially it was made famous through American psychologist Stanley Milgram as he completed experiments which he reported in **"The Small World Problem"** published in "Psychology Today" in 1967. His studies led to the theory of six degrees of separation. While there are numerous writings on how ideas and beliefs travel through groups of people, at the individual level, we are going to focus on how to utilize its techniques throughout the firm.

Once the firm has incorporated a number of the balanced scorecard tools described in this book, it can begin to implement advanced tools that leverage the perspectives of people, processes, customers and finance. This is one of those tools.

In order to use this tool successfully, the firm should determine how to identify and strengthen its networks.

Organizational Network Analysis identifies the organization's network and ties. Within any organization, there are always strong and weak ties. The strong ties are the formal links within the organization, the ties that match the organization's hierarchy from manager to staff to administration. Weak ties are the informal, loose connections that occur outside of the org chart. In utilizing ONIT, it is important to understand that it is the weak ties between the networks control the diffusion of ideas and beliefs between the networks. The people who are the weak tie connectors within and between organizations are known as **Marginals**. Just like cutting-edge Fashionistas in the fashion-trade, **Marginals are the first adopters within any organization.**

These are the staff members who first brought in iPods, who first started using software (Maya, Rhino, Sketchup, Photoshop, etc), not supported by the firm. The Marginal is not just an Early-adopter, a marginal is a pre-Early first adopter. The attraction of ideas to Marginals is necessary for infusing innovations through networks that are frequented by the Early Adopters. Marginals find the openings in networks which are usually closed. The Marginal, as first adopter, must sell the process to the next early adopter.

Marginals are the diffusion adopters. They can be young, old, connected or disenfranchised. Their marginal status is defined by their reaction to the incumbent technology and the process innovation. Marginals and their role in diffusion will come up again in our review of CAD.

Marginals

In order to avoid a commoditization of services, the design firm must develop tools and products which differentiate them from other firms. Successful application of business process differentiation will generate customer attraction. The following questions will help identify innovations:

1) How can a firm select and nurture a process innovation into a new business process that will help set it apart from other design firms?

2) What are the different diffusion rates for process innovations throughout an architecture firm?

3) Are there ONIT tools that can be used to maximize diffusion?

4) How can a firm build a value chain among clients and consultants that creates a climate of innovation and success for diffusion?

5) How can a firm seek out and invest properly in a process innovation?

How can a firm select and nurture a process innovation into a new business process?

"The business enterprise has only two functions: marketing and innovation. It is not necessary for a business to grow bigger; but it is necessary that it constantly grow better"

-Peter Drucker

What is a business process innovation? Innovation is defined as creating value through the implementation of a new idea. A process innovation is a change in the way a product or service is created and distributed. Process innovation involves changing the way a company does things in order to do them better.

Within an architectural firm, a process innovation is any change to the existing business processes that support that organization. Project delivery is a common business process.

Project Delivery

An architectural firm designs and creates contract drawings for construction. Twenty-five years ago this work was performed by trained drafters and architects who drew by hand.

Market-ready Computer Aided Drafting (CAD) became widely available in 1982 with the combined advent of AutoCAD (marketed by Autodesk) and the IBM Personal Computer. This combination helped AutoCAD sell over 50,000 copies by 1986 (with an estimated 500,000 pirated copies), establishing it as the standard brand for computer-aided architectural construction drawing. By 1995, AutoCAD had eliminated most of the nascent incumbent competition, and 70% of all CAD files were delivered by AutoCAD software. Providing hand drawings in lieu of CAD required charging the client for an additional service.

Looking back at this change, how would a firm know that a delivery shift was about to occur? Were there clues during the ten year transition from hand- to computer-aided- drawing for managers that would indicate that a process innovation was occurring?

Incumbent Technology

In 1980 Fred A. Stitt published "Systems Drafting: Creative Reprographics for Architects and Engineers". In that book he outlined methods for updating the contract drawing process by using overlays, transparent adhesives (or sticky-backs as those who remember, called them), and multiple use of reprographic copies. Stitt stated that "...virtually all drafting is repeat drafting."

Throughout the book Stitt proposed techniques which minimized hand-drafting and increased production. Presented as an extension of traditional drafting, Stitt's techniques utilized reprographic houses and drawing assembly rather than drafting. Since the current technology was hand drafting, these reprographic techniques would be listed as a product line extension. In 1980, production drafting was assembly hand - drafting complete with mylar sheets and plastic pencil leads, pin-bars, and blueline reprographics from overlaid transparency copies. At the same time, the incumbent technology for computer-aided drafting was evident with now lost brands such as Autotrol and Datacad. The incumbent drafting technology (pin-bar mylar drafting), was just a little less difficult than determining which new CAD technology to invest in. Drafting technology was primed for a disruption.

The existing value stream.
"Effective process innovation can only succeed if it is accompanied by simultaneous effective innovation of the total value chain."--Maurice Holmes, Xerox Corporation

In 1980, most progressive architectural offices used equipment which supported reprographic drafting assembly. Reprographic businesses provided support for transparency overlays. In order to change this value condition and introduce CAD technology, architectural organizations had to risk investment in new and unknown production technology: plotters (with consumable ink media), drafting paper rolls (in lieu of pre-cut sheets), and networking hardware including computers, drafting tablets, and the associated software. New and specialized staff training for both drafting input and drawing output was required. During this early phase, the risk-reward formula was uncertain. **In 1980, computers were still specialty tools**. Some firms already had large investments in word-processing computers for small document processes including specifications and correspondence. The idea of incorporating a new set of expensive machines, capable only of performing a single activity was viewed as a questionable expense.

During the time of Stitt's book, early eighties, the reprographics support chain was supporting the overlay drafting industry. Intermediate reproducible copies of originals, known as sepias for their tone quality, were produced to provide different domain documents such as reflected ceiling plans, dimension plans, and the like. By the late eighties, the reprographics support chain had changed. Blueprinters were now supporting floppy disk transfer of CAD drawing files. They understood the still problem-riddled CAD processes and were able to help firms store and plot files from computer media.

Additionally, **non-CAD software typically came preloaded on the same computers** the CAD drafters used, and architects started making use of this available spreadsheet and word-processing software along with drafting software. By this point the return on CAD investment became more predictable; and the location of CAD on the adoption curve reached an even higher level. Clients were now demanding CAD documents, and CAD training and expertise was a requirement for all new staff hires.

By the early nineties, it seemed that clear that hand drafting's era had passed.

Stitt's Reprographic Assembly Method for drawing delivery had simply been hand-drafting's ten-year brand extension. Why didn't Fred Stitt's Reprographic Assembly methods last longer in practice? A view from within would have validated his efforts; both clients and firms clearly supported its goals. How could the architectural firm in 1982 determine whether it should invest 1983's money into additional Reprographic equipment or risk wasting time and money on something new called CAD? Or, perhaps, not do anything at all?

TRIZ

In Russian, it's Teoriya Resheniya Izobretatelskikh Zadatch, "TRIZ." In English it's "**The Theory of Inventive Problem Solving**," or just **TRIZ** (properly pronounced "TREES") TRIZ was conceived and developed by **Genrich Altshuller**, a Russian patent examiner. After reviewing thousands of patents and supporting documentations, Altshuller discovered that out of thousands of solutions, there were a just a small number of problem-solving principles that were repeatedly used and reused across many different areas of invention and innovation.

He described these **problem-solving principles as "operators,"** and realized that by using these operators complex problems could be solved. These operators served as patterns for problem solving and understanding what Altshuller called "**technological evolution**". He categorized these processes into eight categories:

1. Processes pass through stages of evolution and are replaced by others.

2. Processes evolve toward their ideal operating process, known as Ideality.

3. Process elements evolve non-uniformly, and a system is frequently held back by a significant contradiction or problem in one of its subsystems or components.

4. Processes become more dynamic and controllable over time.

5. Processes tend to become more complex prior to becoming simpler.

6. Processes evolve with alternating matched and mismatched components.

7. Processes evolve toward the increased use of automatic features (or fields).

8. Processes evolve in the direction of decreased human involvement.

Ideality

TRIZ's Law of Increasing Ideality, states that technical processes evolve toward increasing stages that bring them closer to becoming an ideal process or "Ideality".

All processes contain useful and non-useful activities and all business processes evolve. According to TRIZ, these processes evolve toward an Ideal state. When the short term result of improving an existing business process is an increase in less beneficial effects, the process will accept a trade-off. The Ideality process drives process design to eliminate trade-offs. The ideal final result may be a process where a beneficial function is created that totally replaces the existing process. For example, the ideal evolution of bank tellers to ATMs to debit cards could be seen as an evolution to greater Ideality.

One rule of thumb is to think of Ideality as the useful functionality of a process subtracting the negative factors that diminish its usefulness, divided by the costs to create the overall value. The CAD/Drawing Assembly conundrum Ideality would have been measured by "Drawing Output" minus "Time spent creating drawings" divided by "Expenditures needed (vacuum presses, computers, consumables, etc.) to produce output. The perfect "Ideality" would be a system that delivers a quotient as close to "1" as the formula can create.

Four Technology Phases:

Technological systems evolve through four phases of an S-curve. TRIZ outlines it as follows:

1)   **Infancy, or pre-market phase**, this is where the rate of the system's development phase is relatively slow.

2)   **Rapid Growth**, this is where the system enter s the market and it pace of adoption rapidly escalates, almost exponentially.

3)   **Maturity**, this is the top of the curve, where the system slows down and levels off.

The final phase is –

4)   **Decline**, where a system saturates the market.

Innovation Levels

In order to understand where the system is in its evolution phase, it's helpful to look at what Atschuller described as "innovation levels."

1)   A **component** intended for the innovation is used.

2)   **Existing system is slightly modified**. Solution is transferred from a similar

system.

3)   At least **one principal system's component is radically changed or eliminated**.

4)   A **new system is developed** using interdisciplinary approaches.

5)   **Pioneering innovation occurs**.

In reviewing the innovation levels, the process innovation of CAD was a **type 5**

innovation.

Process Innovation within a project-based professional services organization occurs at

three levels.

1) the Individual level,

2) the Project level, and

3) the Organizational level.

Innovations utilized at each level can convey benefits as **externalities** to other

levels. For example, if a staff member at the individual level learns a new software

program on his/her own time, that knowledge becomes an externality to the project and the organization. Subsequently, if the organization or project trains an individual in a new technology, tool or technique, that individual can take the training as intrinsic knowledge to another firm. In LEED certification, individuals can qualify as LEED certified. Projects also carry LEED certification. Organizationally, LEED services can be supported for individuals and projects alike.

Process innovation needs to be actively nurtured through SNA in order to be successful. And that that nurturing must include market incentives at the firm level, the project level and individual level.

Marginals pick up a new tool, or consign a new use to the tool, and then pass it to the next adopter phase.

How a firm can use TRIZ

A firm can use TRIZ to identify a business process primed to become an innovation process by creating an ideality measure. The less-than-satisfactory effects that an incumbent process generates will evolve to overwhelm its useful effects. For pre-CAD processes, the harmful effects of reprographic assembly began to match the harmful effects of learning a new drafting system.

However, the potential useful effects of CAD were not being realized. The Marginals felt they were being given the opportunity to learn something new and potentially more useful than reprographic assembly. Additionally, the CAD processes were more individual and exclusive. **By combining TRIZ with SNA, Computer Aided Design appealed to the Marginals within an organization who saw the continued**

dependence on old technology as a waste of time and energy. The Marginals are the socially disenfranchised or members of the organization with numerous weak ties to other staff members, and not part of the existing value chain. They asked, "Why draw a line on a paper hard copy, when we can draw lines that could be stored and copied over and over in infinite ways?"

These early adopters were similar to the present staff that began to use Ipods and mp3 players over CDs. Following **diffusion theory; the paste-ups and reprographics paved the way for CAD, as they helped architects look at creating construction drawings in a different way.** Reprographic assembly was an interim step that made the next step to computer drawings acceptable. Soon, reprographic drafting was seen to be old-fashioned. Why spend additional money to make reprographics more seamless? Maintaining their existing investment in flatbeds and vacuum presses, firms created a budget to invest in the next new thing.

Back to Marginals

As discussed earlier, Marginals control diffusion. Demonstrating their new adoption to their weak-tie peers generates the buzz that propels the innovation. If the innovation simplifies existing processes, while creating opportunity for future growth of possibilities of the process, additional adopters will diffuse the innovation. In the case of CAD acceptance in the design industry, once adopters started jumping onboard, firms not considering CAD felt that they might be left behind.

We've identified **Marginals**—those staff members with a number of tenuous ties to other Marginals in other organizations. Like other new ideas, process innovations are adopted relatively earlier by Marginals. The dichotomy "strength of weak ties" suggests that once the process is adopted by Marginals, their weak ties spread the innovation to the rest of the professional community. However it is not the centrality or marginality that most affects the rate of diffusion, but the presence of the weak ties themselves.

Weak ties and diversity outside of the organization (architects meeting with non-architects for example, using the surf parking lot metaphor) help connect otherwise unconnected groups and help to spread an innovation. Especially risky innovations diffuse more quickly if they are adopted early by individuals with many weak ties. However, relying on weak ties alone to generate the diffusion necessary to engender true innovation will result in a slower rate of diffusion.

Management needs to keep in mind that potentially risky innovations adopted early on by individuals with few weak ties will generate a slower rate of diffusion and be initially confined to a few interconnected cliques or small specialty groups.

How should the manage **Marginals**? Should they actively use them as vehicles of innovation? What happens if a Marginal is really not a marginal? To identify, consider existing project related processes. Is a weak tie going to get excited about a process that everyone is already using? No. To generate excitement a new idea must be shared. It's the newness, the gee-whiz factor. If it's new, this novel idea travels. Think of how a rumor travels through strong ties. In strong ties everyone knows the person being gossiped about, so the diffusion is hindered. Each strong tie says, "I don't want to talk about that person, because he or she may hear about it". With strong ties, the rumor stops. But introduce weak ties and the rumor continues unabated. If you factor in the media, the rumor goes spreads unabated.

A similar transition is taking place with **Revit,** Autodesk's Building Information Modeling (BIM) software. The **Marginals are key to the diffusion**. Autodesk understands this as they actively support the creation of Revit User Groups (RUGs) in most large cities. For the last few years the RUGs were key to the diffusion within the architecture world as marginal first adopters shared user secrets with each other. At each monthly meeting, revit users would share ideas, lessons learned, and best practices as well as dinner and drinks with other first adopter users. Autodesk itself would often send reseller staff to display hidden features of the software to the gathered marginals. Often missing from these meetings however, were the diverse industries which are crucial to making an innovation diffuse even further. For its next innovation, Autodesk should look to inviting contractors, owners, artists, graphic designers, even comic book designers to help the diffusion.

Summary

In summary, firms should explore and dedicated diffusion programs which could target betweeness in first and early adopters in order to promote more rapid and extensive spread.

So how does a firm develop an adoption cycle?

Develop and Adoption Cycle

Internal and external customers

External customers

As we've discussed so far in this book, the architecture firm has many customers. Its external customers are its clients, contractors and agencies. Clients as customers directly buy services from the design firm. In the process of providing those services the firm also provides services to secondary external customers including contractors, who are now working for the client, and agencies, who are providing code and life-safety appraisal of the firm's deliverables for the client. While an unhappy primary customer such as a client can cause problems for a firm, unsatisfied secondary customers in contracting and agency roles can cause even more significant issues for the design team.

To help **diffuse an innovation**, the design firm should consider how the innovation can help deliver a better product to its primary and secondary external customers and how to use the strength of these customers as weak ties to promote the innovation beyond its industry.

1980's early adopter

For example, in the 1980's, the early-adopter design firms were sold CAD as an additional service to their client base. They did this by developing the support of their secondary customers, the contractors and agencies, to help sell the innovation through weak ties to their clients. Contractors sold the innovation of CAD as a way to provide

soft-copy as-built drawings for facility archiving: the client owned a set of electronic CAD

documents of its campus for it facility managers.

Agencies also promoted CAD as an archival system. Instead of warehousing

permit drawings of thousands of local jurisdiction projects, some agencies would

request copies of a design firm's electronic drawings, which allowed a superior indexing

and referencing database, with the ability to provide copies as needed to future design

firms or contractors for existing projects.

Selling to Internal Customers

The internal customers for the firm include -

1) project team members,

2) back-of-house administration,

3) outside-of-project-team organization members,

4) consultant-team members and

5) supplier-team members.

Selling each of these customers is necessary to building a support base for the

innovation.

Project Team Members.

The project team comes to the game with pre-set demands and requirements. The team's project manager should know how to produce the required deliverables with minimal support from management. However, if the firm is trying to nurture a process innovation, it will have to provide incentives and safety-nets to mitigate the risk to the project team. If using the innovation will place the project in jeopardy either in schedule or budget, the firm must provide support and incentives to continue with the innovation.

Back of house

Administration will not support an innovation if it disrupts its daily processes without incentive. In order to make the innovation easy to promote, consider applying adoption considerations: such as helping write new proposals, pricing methodology and billing and invoicing support. Identifying the innovation as a separate product or delivery line will help calculate and manage time efficiently.

Outside-of-project-team organization members

These are team members within the firm that are not directly working on the project utilizing the innovation. The firm should support these firm members by continuing to support their projects and their roles. The firm should outline tasks within the non-innovation projects that could benefit from the innovation. For example, the revit innovation team could build a model of one of the non-revit project's components

Consultant-team members

The consultant-team members are often the most neglected partners in the innovation diffusion. If we're forcing an innovation on all the team, then we have to support all members of the consultants- the execs, the administration staff (billing, etc), as well as the project managers.

Supplier-team members.

Suppliers are only second to the consultant team for neglect. We should consider how to actively engage the suppliers (these are the reprographic houses, the specialty consultants (spec writers, etc)

Identifying and diffusing an innovation
Building Information Modeling (BIM)

As outlined above, building information modeling (BIM) is now moving from the first adopter phase into early adopter. As of early 2008, fewer than 10% of architectural firms used BIM exclusively in their production of construction documents. Now in early 2009, over 40% are listing active BIM projects. However, even with this rate of diffusion, marginals are still the current experts in BIM programs such as Revit.

To confirm Marginal status, just ask a manager at any architectural firm how high-maintenance their Revit staff is-

"Don't get them mad, If they don't show up, or work strange hours an executive at a mid-sized west coast studio told me recently (Our BIM consultant wanted time and half to work on Presidents Day (even though he was a consultant). We let him have the day off, without pay.

Even with 60% penetration, BIM is still the gee-whiz misfit that the firm uses to tell its clients that it is keeping up with the times. But is BIM worth the investment? Can another black box hooked up to kids wearing headphones create better documents than the last black box?

Diffusion and opportunity risk

High diffusion – Low Risk –the opportunity cost of using the innovation against not using it. Project failure and its repercussions. **Innovation fatigue**, wasting time on learning a software which will not be used again.

The innovation must first solve a problem the existing technology (incumbent) does not, and do it with low enough risk that an investment innovation, at the individual, project or organizational level cannot be too great that it cannot be abandoned. Disruptive process innovations may also adaptations of existing processes that are easier to use than existing tools. The performance of these disruptive innovations often lets a new group of users (for CAD software, the users may be managers who never learned CAD) accomplish necessary tasks more easily and conveniently than using an incumbent technology.

How then, does the individual, project team, and organization determine if a new process based activity is an innovation that deserves support?

Innovation can be defined as the commercial application of a new piece of cost-saving technology. It can take the form of a change in the way a product or service is manufactured, created, or distributed concept suggesting that customers first enter a market at different times, depending on their attitude to innovation and new products, and their willingness to take risks.

The design firm can utilize balanced metrics to identify and pursue innovative processes.

It can also use the same metrics to confirm existing successful processes as part of the RISMI review process.

Innovative Firm KPIs and Metrics.

Initiative	Perspective	Objective	Lag Measure	Lead Measure	Target
Innovation	Financial	Build diverse teams into fee breakdowns.			
	Customers	Introduce Diverse Team to Clients			
	Processes	Integrate new staff through existing studios			
	People	Hire cognitively diverse staff			

The next part

Customers and Financial Perspectives

In part 2 we review the Customers and Financial perspectives, and explore

balanced metrics to align them with the People and Process perspectives, and create

metrics to support a sustainable design firm.